Invisible Colored White

Being White in a Black World

Richard Rizzo

Invisible Colored White 2

For Dov and Nick

Table of Contents

CHILDHOOD

Beginnings

It started when my mother remarried. Until then I had been living a pretty conventional life. I was a normal kid growing up in Brooklyn after World War Two. My neighborhood, Bensonhurst, consisted mostly of Italians and Jews. There were others; I remember French and Irish families, but I can't recall having any Protestant friends, though I couldn't swear to that. At the time, none of that seemed to matter to any of us. In fact, the Jewish-Italian thing kind of worked for me. Every Saturday I was a Shabbos Goy; I got to stuff my hand in the pine-nut jar just for turning out the lights in Abe's house. If my hand was unwashed no one seemed to notice.

I don't remember worrying about much in those days. If I wanted an egg cream I just went over to the candy store and asked for it. The owner kept track of what I'd had and my father paid for it at the end of the week. I was the only kid I knew with that kind of deal. Any day of the week I could have gone in there and walked away with enough candy to send the whole block into a sugar high. But I never took advantage of my situation because I knew, if I did, it would have made my father look like a bigger sucker than the touch he was known to be all over the neighborhood.

There was a reason I had this special deal. My father didn't live with us. I lived on 68th near Bay Parkway, and my father lived on 61st near 18th Avenue. Maybe I wasn't as carefree as I said, due to my parents being divorced, but that wasn't a big thing. After the war, a lot of kids had fathers who had been away, and some had fathers who never came back. My dad sat on a beach in the Pacific for the whole war. When he came home, he just moved back into the house he was born in, and he stayed there for the rest of his life. I dealt with it by making myself believe that his not living with us was a temporary thing, like he had just gone around the corner for a pack of smokes and he was expected back any minute.

When, as an adult, I asked my mother why she had divorced my father, she looked me right in the eye, paused as though she was deciding whether or not to tell the truth, and said, "You know what he was like: he was a good man; he was just too passive. I couldn't live with a man who had such little initiative. It would have been like living with a television set: you could turn it on, and time would pass, and nothing real would have happened."

I asked her why, if that was true, she had married him in the first place. This time the long pause didn't involve looking me in the eye. All she could come up with was, "As I said, he was a good man."

For many years I wondered if she couldn't

bring herself to tell me that I was an accident, and that my father had done what men were supposed to do in those days when accidents happened. As an adult I checked their marriage certificate, and it appears they were actually married nine months before I was born. So why she married him remains a mystery. In any case, that is a minor matter in my life when compared with the bomb that fell when I was nine.

My old life came to an end in 1949. My mother had joined the Communist Party, and she had fallen in love with one of the leaders. In those days there were lots of Communists running around. One of them, Vito Marcantonio, a guy my mom had worked for, was even elected to Congress. What made my mom's love affair a big deal was that the guy she was in love with was black. Up until that time I had never even spoken with a black person. I might have seen one on the street, but that was about it. They didn't go into people's houses in Bensonhurst, except maybe to clean, and I didn't know anyone who had a cleaning lady.

I started to learn about my new life the day my mother took me on the Sea Beach line across the bridge into Manhattan. The way I knew something was up was that she had let me stand by myself in the front of the first car where the big coupling wheel was, so I could look out at the tracks and make believe I was driving. We changed at Times Square for the IRT and we took it way uptown. I had never done that before. We got off, and I was in a world I had never even imagined existed: a place called

Harlem.

We went into an apartment building and the next thing I knew I was shaking hands with this bald-headed black man. A few days later my mother asked if it was okay for her to marry him. What was I supposed to say? *Sure go ahead, ruin my life.* What I did say was something like, "If you really love him, mom, then go ahead." I wasn't being brave. Actually I am a coward; I should have said what I was thinking, but the chicken in me wouldn't let it out.

This is something I inherited from my father. It's down there in the DNA, and there's not much you can do about it except live with it. It's not such a bad thing really; I've come to believe it's why I survived. Probably in all biological history there have been two evolutionary tracks: one in which the bulls go at it, and the winner gets the girl; the other track, the quieter one, is the one in which the girl finds the guy hiding in the bushes. She sees he's scared; she likes him because she's scared too. Anyway, for better or worse, I'm the guy in the bushes. I've come to believe that we cowards are just as necessary for the survival of the species as the heroic types who start marching at the first beat of any drum.

I'm getting ahead of myself. I have a tendency to cut to the chase. This is a good thing as long as you don't miss details that would have taken you in a more interesting direction. So let me back up a bit.

My mother's house

I remember saying, "If you exist, strike me dead." I was looking up at the sky when I said it, staring straight at a big puffball of a cloud that had caught my attention. It was a smart-ass thing to do, considering where the challenge was directed. I waited a while; when nothing happened I figured I had my answer.

Then about an hour later a huge black cloud in the shape of a man riding a horse caught my attention. He was wearing one of those Kaiser helmets with the point on top. One of his arms was raised over his head, and in that arm, which stretched all the way from Coney Island to Redhook, he held a sword that could have demolished most of Brooklyn. The shape was too perfect to be an accident. As soon as I saw it I knew the war was over.

My father was stationed on an island in the Pacific. Its exact location was a military secret. The only thing I knew for sure was that it was nothing but sand and palm trees. I had learned this from the letter he wrote me. Inside the envelope there was a necklace. He made the necklace out of seashells that looked just like the conchiglie pasta that Aunt Mary made with ricotta. The only difference was that these shells had brown flecks on top, and underneath, instead of a curl that went into itself, the real shells had a slit that made them look like they had been closed with stitches.

I don't know why he gave me that necklace. It wasn't something a boy could wear. I kept it in my dresser; every once in a while I would take it out to hold. I would grab it like I was holding the reins of a horse, and I would squeeze each shell with my thumb; then I would push the shell over my trigger finger to make room for the next one. I would do that, one by one, until I had come back to the beginning.

That afternoon I heard about the Japanese surrender on the radio. For the rest of the day I was in the center of a hurricane of celebrating people: none of them with a clue about the most important thing that had happened. Being able to tell the future had to be a bigger deal than the end of a war – even a world war.

My excitement lasted all day, but by the time I got into bed I was tired of trying to find omens. When I woke up the next morning I knew it was just a big coincidence. I had to get going. I needed my mother's permission to go swimming before she left for work, or Aunt Mary would make me stick around the house the whole day. I threw on a tee shirt and dungarees and ran into the kitchen barefoot. Grandpa was alone at the table breaking off chunks of stale Italian bread and dropping them into his bowl.

Sometimes, when we were out of cereal, I would have Grandpa's kind of breakfast. I liked bread soaked in milk, but I couldn't see eating it every day the way he did. As far as I was concerned even variety packs got boring after a while. But Grandpa never seemed to want anything but his bread and milk. He was thick and stubborn like that. His real name was Guiseppi Manosia. No one ever called him that: the neighbors called him Joe, and everyone in the family called him *capotosto*, which in our kind of Italian meant *hardhead*.

He was sitting with his back to me. From where I was standing I couldn't see any neck. There was just this white haired cube set on top of his curved shoulders. He was a squat barrel of a man with shoulders that had been worn down over the years. When he walked he waddled from side to side like a refrigerator being walked across the kitchen floor. I think he had something wrong with one of his legs but he never spoke of it. It didn't matter because speed was not his thing. Neither was talking: he usually grunted or made some soft sound. Sometimes he moved his body to show what he meant. If that didn't work he would shout. None of it did any good, quiet or loud, no one listened to him. Mostly he just shrugged; I guess he figured the world had been created to give him a hard time.

Aunt Mary came into the kitchen. She was short and solidly built like Grandpa. Though she wasn't fat, her waist didn't curve in to her hips the way my mother's did. My mother and her sister were the same weight but my mother was taller and she didn't have to wear girdles. Aunt Mary wasn't as pretty as my mother: her eyes bulged out and her hair always looked like it had been glued in place. I noticed her eyes were a little more watery than usual.

She said, "Once and for all, it's in her name and she's not going to sign."

She was using English; usually she spoke Italian with Grandpa, but when she was mad she always used English. As little as Grandpa liked using Italian, he hated using English even more. Grandpa acted like he hadn't heard her, answering me instead like the two of us were having a conversation.

"It's my money."

This was a very old argument they were about to have. Maybe the details might change each time, but the basic idea stayed the same. Grandpa had been a bricklayer. He had worked on a lot of famous buildings, even the Empire State. Now that he was retired, he got some kind of check every month that he turned over to Aunt Mary. Grandpa didn't know how to read and write; just signing his name was a big deal for him. You could see on his face the pain it caused him when he tried to make the lines that were supposed to stand for his name. Aunt Mary took care of the bills and the other business of the family.

Grandpa was always about to make a big killing. Every day of his life he had some big plan going. His latest idea was to rent a little strip of land that ran between the BMT tracks and put a bunch of his Catania paesans to work growing tomatoes there. In exchange for letting them work his land they would keep half of what they grew. That was the way things were done in Sicily, and Grandpa figured it would work here with the BMT land he wanted to rent.

It didn't seem like such a bad idea to me, but Aunt Mary and Grandma were against it. To get his plan going, Grandpa needed to take out a loan on the house and they wouldn't let him. His hands were tied because the house was in Grandma's name. All he could do was yell and slam things around, which was exactly what he would end up doing whenever the subject came up.

He was about to do that now. I could tell by the way he opened his mouth; it was as if he couldn't believe that anyone, let alone his own flesh and blood, could treat him this way. It was tough for him to pull this act off because he always acted this way. But he was doing his best, making his face red and opening his eyes wide. Finally a high-pitched roar came out of his throat. It didn't sound like Italian, not even Sicilian; it was more like the sound a pig might make if you stuck it with a spear. Next, he did something I had never seen him do before. He went over to the cabinet where he kept a jug of the wine he made in the basement, and he poured himself one of the big glasses. He started to drink it, and Mary shouted, "Ubriacone."

I had never seen Grandpa drink in the morning, much less from a big glass like that. True, he always had wine later in the day, usually with a meal. He often drank a lot but he was never drunk, or at least if he was you couldn't tell the difference. Aunt Mary shouted it again, and Grandpa just looked at her and finished off the glass. Then he gave out with a loud cluck of his tongue and poured himself another glass. This was more than Mary could take. She went over to the counter where he was standing and grabbed for the jug. He grabbed it too, and the two of them started a tug of war.

I was scared. I had seen them argue many times. It was more or less the only way they related. But this was different; they were actually fighting. Grandpa had both hands on the jug and he had pulled it against his body like he was hugging a teddy bear. Aunt Mary still had one hand on the jug, and with the other arm, she hauled off and hit him.

Grandpa screamed like a baby. She had only tapped him on the shoulder; it couldn't have hurt very much, but he acted like she had taken his arm off. He started crying. Tears came down his cheeks; he was acting just like a kid. I was very embarrassed for him.

Luckily, my mother came into the kitchen just then. She took one look at the two of them and yelled, "Stop it. The two of you, stop it right now." Both of them reacted as if they were kids and she was a teacher scolding them. Aunt Mary was the first to speak: "He's pouring wine in him like there's no tomorrow."

My mother didn't pay any attention to this. She went over to Grandpa and handed him a dishtowel so he could wipe his face. I knew my mother was about to leave for work because she turned to me and gave me her look. She could make her face look like the thing she was about to do was so terrible she couldn't bring herself to do it. But it was never terrible enough to stop her.

Grandpa left the kitchen and Aunt Mary started washing the breakfast dishes. The fight was over for now. They wouldn't say another word to each other for the rest of the day and that was another good reason to get out of the house and over to the pool.

My mother was already late for work, but I knew it didn't matter very much. She had a part-time job working at a newspaper called *L'Unita del Popolo.* It wasn't a real newspaper, not like the kind most people read. First of all it was in Italian. Even though there were probably more Italians in Bensonhurst than Rome, the cigar store on 18th Avenue, that had more papers than you could count, didn't sell it. If that wasn't bad enough, it didn't come out every day. I think it came out once a week or maybe even every other week. It was just like my mother to be working on a newspaper that had nothing but old news.

It wasn't like she was a reporter. All she did was take a story that someone had written in English and translate it into Italian. If I know her, she probably got it wrong most of the time too. But they never fired her. I guess they couldn't find anyone else to do the job for what they were paying her.

It wasn't just the newspaper that kept her away from the house; she was always going to meetings too. I don't know what they did at those meetings; the only thing I know for sure is that they smoked a lot. The morning after one of her meetings she would come into the kitchen smelling like a smokestack.

When she bent down to kiss me goodbye, I whispered that I wanted to go swimming and asked her to tell Aunt Mary that it was okay. I figured she didn't have an idea of her own about it, and I wanted to get her on my side before Aunt Mary had a chance to give her opinion. I knew Aunt Mary wouldn't want me to go there alone. Sure enough, Aunt Mary had heard me and she said, "He can't go there by himself, it's too far."

"It's too far," my mother repeated, just like she knew what she was talking about. I knew it wouldn't do any good to argue that I knew the way like the back of my hand. As far as Aunt Mary was concerned, when I was out of her sight, I was always in great danger. My best chance was to try another idea so I said, "If I can get Abe's brother to take us, can I go?"

My mother, who usually gave in to me, looked at Aunt Mary as if to say: *why not?* The fight with Grandpa must have exhausted Aunt Mary because she said, "If they stay an hour, maybe. I don't want him in the water all day. He'll get polio." For Aunt Mary *polio* stood for everything bad that could happen. As soon as she said it I knew I had won. Even if Abe's brother wouldn't do it, I would find a way.

No one was home at Abe's, so I went to the pool on my own. It wasn't exactly a pool: the water was too shallow for swimming. It was really just a big fountain, a wading pool with concrete sprinklers around the edges, surrounded by an iron bar fence. To get inside you had to wade through a footbath. Everyone avoided the chemical footbath by holding on to the bars of the fence and jumping across.

In winter they drained the pool and we played dodge ball in there. It was great for that because you were trapped and you had to stay on your toes. In summer, we just sat over the sprinklers and watched the older guys do tricks on the iron bars.

Grandma Manosia

Grandma Manosia was screaming again. In my whole life, I had never seen her out of bed, and I had never heard her stop complaining. Dr. Bonadio came over to check up on her every once in a while, but we all knew he had given up on her a long time ago. Other doctors had come and gone too; none of them seemed to be able to say exactly what was wrong with her. The medicine cabinet was full of stuff they had tried on her without solving her problem. You would think that after a few weeks, or a month or two, a person would go numb from the pain, but she managed to go on for years treating every new day like she was hurting for the first time.

My mother was in the kitchen. I asked if she thought Grandma would ever stop screaming. "She wants attention, Richie. I'm not saying she doesn't feel anything; I'm sure she does. It's just that she knows that if she keeps it up long enough, sooner or later, Mary will come into her bedroom to take care of her."

I could see what my mother was getting at. In a way Aunt Mary was making it easy for Grandma to keep on with her screaming. It was nice of my mother to point this out because it got us off the hook for not doing anything. I said, "If they cured her of whatever is wrong with her she would probably catch something else just to get our attention."

I knew I wasn't supposed to be saying things

like that, but it was the truth, and I figured my mother wouldn't get mad at me for telling the truth for a change. Sure enough she nodded, and said, "If she had stayed in Italy they would have done things to get rid of *malocchio*. Eventually they would have found a cure that was worse than the pain."

My mother knew from pain. She had been run over by a truck when she was a little girl. Luckily, the only part of her that was damaged was her arm. She had a huge scar that went all the way from her wrist to above her elbow. Her arm was always a little crooked. Most people would have tried to hide it. Not my mother; she wore short sleeved blouses whenever she had a chance. I had never heard her complain about it. I asked her if her arm hurt her and she said, "It's just a little ache that comes and goes. The doctors call it *bursitis*."

One thing you had to give her; she was brave. She never let trouble worry her or keep her from doing what she wanted to do. I was a lot more like my old man: most of the time I would be thinking about what could go wrong.

The way she went out during the day, and left me with Aunt Mary, made a lot of people feel she thought too highly of herself. She didn't think she was better than other people; it was just that she had her own ideas about what was right. The problem was her ideas were different than the way the rest of Bensonhurst thought. I liked her for that, but it did make it harder for everyone to understand why she did what she did. In a way she was like Grandma Manosia: the two of them didn't mind making it tough on other people if it meant getting what they wanted.

Achilles Colombino Rizzo

My mother told me that her family was from Catania, Sicily. Beyond that, I know nothing of her family's history. The earliest public record I have of my mother's family is her birth certificate. She was born on Valentine's Day, 1918, in Holyoke, Massachusetts. The spelling of the family name on that document is Manazio, not the Manosia that appears in later official records relating to my mother.

The only relative born in Italy for whom I have specific documentation is my father's father, Achilles. He was born in Amantea, a little village on the Tyrrhenian Sea, in Calabria, Southern Italy. Here is a translation of the Registrar's statement of his birth.

On the 27th day of September, 1884, at 11:40 A.M., in the Town Hall, before me personally appeared Anna Benigno, twenty-eight years old, farmer, domiciled in Amantea, who handed over to me a baby of male sex apparently two days old with no identification on him, and declared to me that today, at three A.M., in Colongio Street near the house number 24, she found this baby laying on his back with his hands inside swaddling clothes, and that she named the said baby Achille Colombino.

The declarant thereafter requested she be allowed to keep the above-mentioned baby, promising to raise and take care of him as well as to answer for him whenever asked by the authorities, and having found nothing against such request I granted it and gave this baby to the declarant, Anna Benigno, wife of Guido Gennaro.

(Illegible) Raffaele, sixty-three years old, sailor, and (Illegible) Antonio, fifty-four years old, laborer, both residing in this town, were present as witnesses to the foregoing and to this instrument. This instrument was read to the present persons and then was signed by me only, for the others stated that they were unable to sign.

As far as I know, Achilles' subsequent life is undocumented until December 3, 1895, when he appears among the passengers arriving in New York on a ship named the *California* from Naples. Achille Columbrino, [sic] 11 years old, is listed on the ship's manifest along with a Livia Guida, 24. In the 1900 census, Olivia Guida is listed as a sister-in-law living in a Lower East Side household headed by Pasquale Rizzo. Also enumerated in that census is Achilles, by then 14, listed as the oldest of the four Rizzo children. Pasquale reported that he had been living in the U.S. for seven years at the time of the census. His wife, Maria, having been married to him for seventeen years, is reported as having arrived in the U.S. three years earlier, at the same time as Olivia, Achilles, and the other three children (daughters, aged 2, 7, and 10).

Was Pasquale my grandfather's father, and if so, who was his mother? Surely, Maria wouldn't have abandoned him on the street in Amantea. The woman who said she found Achilles, Anna Benigno, was married at the time. Why had she agreed to care for him?

Having spent time in Southern Italian villages, I am certain everyone in the village knew the true story. A day after arriving to visit friends in Gratteri, a small village in Sicily, I went into a bakery to buy some rolls. The shopkeeper, someone I was meeting for the first time, asked me where in Palermo my family had lived. Though the story about me was slightly off, my maternal grandfather was from Catania not Palermo; I was sure that by sunset everyone in town would know the corrected version.

Had a barren marriage resulted in an undocumented adoption? Or had Pasquale strayed and then brought his illegitimate son to America? Was the original surname given to the child, *Little Columbus,* significant? One thing is certain: Pasquale embraced the boy as his son. My grandfather Achilles Colombino, became Achilles Rizzo in America. His children—Patrick, George, Mary, and my father, Arthur—were all given one of the most common surnames in Italy.

My father comes home

Grandpa Rizzo's house was on the corner. It seemed like everyone who lived on 61st Street had come by at some time that day. I heard one woman say, "Georgie must have got lost." My Uncle George (everyone called him Georgie) had gone to pick up my father. Someone yelled, "No, they just stopped for a beer." I had already gone to 18th Avenue and back about ten times, and I had just started to make one more trip when I saw the car. My uncle was driving. Sitting next to him was a man I was pretty sure was my father. Not knowing your old man was a pretty stupid thing but he had been gone so long I really wasn't sure what he looked like. The only memory I had was from the album pictures of him. The man sitting next to Georgie looked a little like the guy in my album but his eyes seemed deader. The big smile on his face couldn't hide that look in his eyes. As soon as he got out of the car he walked right up to me, picked me up, and gave me a kiss. Being picked up and kissed like a baby made me feel even weirder than I already felt. With everyone watching I didn't want to pull away, so I kept hugging him like I meant it, even though I felt like I was hanging on to a stranger.

It was a pretty good performance. When he put me down I could tell people were impressed. Then he walked up to his father and shook his hand. Grandpa Rizzo had stayed back, which was the way he was. You would think that having a son come back from a war would be the kind of thing that would make you a little emotional but, as far as I could tell, he wasn't feeling a thing. After he shook Grandpa's hand he moved on to Grandma. She was standing on the porch with her arms stretched out in front of her waiting for him. This was the way she always stood when she knew someone was coming to greet her. But unlike Grandpa she had a good reason. You had to bump into her hands to let her know where you were. Then, if you were a kid, she would bend forward so you could kiss her on the cheek. She didn't have to bend for my father; she just turned her face to the side, he kissed her and gave her a long hug.

Everyone went inside except Grandma, my father, and me. I stayed down on the sidewalk and watched. They must have thought I was inside too because, without looking back, my father helped Grandma get through the door. Then he stayed on the porch for a few seconds and he did the thing that made me sure it was him.

My father had a habit: he would put the knuckles of two fingers against something solid and hold his hand on it a few seconds. Usually it was a doorknob or a light switch but just about anything would do: a wall, a table, even the refrigerator. He would just hold his hand on the thing and then he would let go and move on. Sometimes he would walk away a few steps; then he would come back and do the whole *mishegas* over again. It was strange: so strange that I couldn't figure out why he did it. For all I knew he was getting some kind of charge from the objects he was touching. Probably it didn't have any meaning at all; he liked routine and having a compulsion to touch familiar objects must have been comforting to him in some way. He still had his fingers against the doorknob when I reached the top of the stoop. Now that I was sure that he was my father I could say what I was thinking. I told him I had to get back to my mother's. He said he would walk me over there.

On the way there I asked him what he was going to do. He looked at me as though he hadn't understood and then he said, "I'm going to take the test for the TA." A few of my friends had fathers who were policemen or firemen, but most of the Italian fathers I knew of, who worked for the city, were in the Department of Sanitation. Having a father who was a garbage collector was not something you could brag about so I was glad he had decided to work for the transit authority.

I knew you had to take a test for a job like that and I asked him if he thought he would pass. I figured he would do well because of the way he wrote. He printed in perfect block letters; he could write better than any of my teachers. A skill like that would be the kind of thing they would be after on the test. He told me they gave points for being in the Navy and that cinched it. He was never over-confident, and if he said he had a good chance that meant it was a sure thing. He would never get my hopes up on a long shot.

As we walked along without saying anything, which was fine with me, I tried to imagine him driving a train or a bus. The more I thought about it the more I could see that it was the perfect job for him. He always paid a lot of attention to time. It wasn't that he got upset if he was late, he just liked to measure things. Keeping track of time was one of his favorite occupations. Right now he was probably thinking, *five minutes to Sixty-eighth and a minute to Bay Parkway.*

Grandpa Rizzo was an optometrist. He had been in the jewelry business but now he just did glasses and watch repairing on the side. Working all day with those little wheels turning bigger wheels, and lenses on top of lenses, would be the kind of thing that would drive you, and your kids, nuts. I guess if my father had gone into the family business I might have ended up measuring things too.

I could see how, even though he was only back a few hours, the rest of my father's life was already all worked out. Grandpa Rizzo had wound him up so tight he never stood a chance of doing something risky. Touching the door knob, measuring the time to Sixty-eighth, and applying for the TA job were all so tied together he couldn't let go of the smallest part of it. If, when we came to Sixty-eighth, there was no street there—if it was just a bunch of empty lots as far as you could see—my old man was so locked in to doing what you were supposed to do, he would just keep walking anyway.

It must have driven my mother crazy. If there was one thing she couldn't do, it was to follow a plan. I couldn't remember ever seeing her go from the start of something straight through to the finish without some kind of major detour. When I tried to imagine the two of them together all I got was Hopalong Cassidy meets Abbott and Costello.

When we reached Aunt Mary's corner he stopped. It was like he had just read some sign on the sidewalk that said: *This is as far as Arthur Rizzo can go.* He crouched down and gave me a hug. There were pictures of him playing sandlot ball in Grandpa Rizzo's album and, squatting there, he looked like he was still catching for New Utrich High. I gave him a hug and he said, "Make sure you stop for a malted."

My father got the job with the transit authority. He drove a bus until the TA found out he had diabetes. They were afraid he might pass out while driving so they put him in a token booth. He would sit in there, all day long, with nothing to do but slide coins around. His knack for keeping track of time, which was great for driving a bus, must have made the time pass more slowly in the cage. On the weekends when I was in Brooklyn, I would ask about his work. He never complained.

The Wedding 1949

My mother had said that a white person and a Negro couldn't get married in New York City. It wasn't clear to me where she got this idea. There probably weren't any laws against it in 1949 in New York but that doesn't mean inter-racial marriages were common. According to an article I read recently in the Journal of Family History only 150 inter-racial marriages were performed in the entire U.S. during the decade of the 40's.

I don't know where they were married; I believe it was Connecticut, but I'm not sure. What I do remember was that a man, a white man, drove my mother, Pete, and myself out of the city. We traveled a long distance and finally pulled up to a big wooden building. I half expected the police to be waiting outside but there were just a few of my mother's friends, people I had never seen before. A lady gave Mom some flowers. It was just a small bouquet, something to hold in one hand. I worried that I should have brought a present but there was nothing to be done about that.

We all went around to the side of the house, up a long outside staircase, and then Mom, Pete, and I, were shown into a small room. Mom was dressed up: she was wearing a new satin dress. It was blue, my favorite color, and when she moved, the light made it look green, like one of those pictures that change when you move them. Pete had on a dark suit, white shirt, and a tie that had brown flowers on it. He was smiling to beat the band; you couldn't miss his gold teeth. The gold looked good against the dark brown skin of his face. Part of me wanted to be ashamed of his teeth because they made him seem like he was old. Another part of me said: *the hell with it; people who think that kind of stuff mattered were jerks.*

A guy came in. I could tell by the way he took charge he was the one (the minister or whatever he was) who was going to marry them. He didn't seem to know them but when he got to me he said, "And you're Richard; your mother and Pete told me about you."

Neither of them had said a word to him so I guessed they must have talked it over on the phone beforehand. I didn't like the idea of this guy knowing about me and me not even knowing what kind of church he ran. I looked at Mom for some kind of explanation but, before she could speak, he told me I could say a few words in the ceremony if I wanted to, or I could just stand there without doing or saying anything. I was glad he didn't think I knew what was supposed to happen.

Now that I knew my part I could relax a little. I told him I didn't want to say anything. Then we went out to a bigger room, and he stood with his back to the wall. The people in there, four or five of them, and us, all gathered around, facing him. He started talking about America: how we all came here from different places. I didn't see what this had to do with marrying people but I figured this was the kind of wedding that you made up as you went along; it didn't have to make a lot of sense. It was pretty clear he didn't know what he was talking about: *the Indians didn't come here; they were here.*

He had gotten to the part I knew. "Do you, Rose Manosia, take Pettis Perry ..." PETTIS PERRY? What kind of name was that? I thought his name was Pete. I almost burst out laughing. So as not to let the laugh out, I looked down and bit my lip. I could taste the blood. If I had caught someone's eye at that moment, even one of the people I didn't know, I would have broken up.

They had gotten as far as the kiss the bride part. My mother was around Pete's height but for some reason she was standing on her toes to kiss him. Pete had his arms around her, holding her, and they had their lips together a long time. Then everyone started clapping like it was a play that had just ended. Everyone acted a little strange then, like they didn't know what to do next.

Right then the only thing I could think of was how to make myself disappear. Of course, to make that impossible my mother had to come over and try to give me a kiss. I turned my head to the side so our lips wouldn't touch, but somehow she managed to plant a big wet kiss square on my lips. I hated the taste of her lipstick.

Then the strangest thing happened: I felt all tingly and I knew I was invisible. One second the only thing I could think of was all the people watching me, and the next second I was sure none of them could see me. Everything still looked the same: the room, my mom, the other people; none of it had changed.

But I wasn't there anymore; I knew because, before, I could feel them pushing in on me. Now that feeling was gone.

My father used to take me to the Fun House in Coney Island. In the Hall of Mirrors, if you stood in a particular spot you could see the people all around you but you couldn't see yourself. I wasn't in the Fun House now but, at that exact moment, I knew that no one in the room could see me. If I was careful I could even move around without being seen. Whenever I saw someone's attention start to move in my direction—it was like a shadow falling off them—I would move out of the way.

I was feeling pretty safe. I inched over to the minister. Sure enough, when I got near, he started to slip away in the other direction. It was like he was afraid of me. This was great; it meant I could go wherever I wanted. I moved all the way to the other side of the room. No one noticed. Then I got over-confident and decided to go back to the center where my mother was standing. To be invisible next to her would be the biggest test.

Suddenly a hand shot out of the crowd and landed on my shoulder. It was the minister. As soon as he touched me I felt all the weight coming back into my body. He bent down and whispered in my ear: "I think you should go over and congratulate Pete."

I swore to myself that I would never push my invisibility that far again. Now, I felt even weirder than when I got the kiss. Instead of being invisible I could feel everyone's eyes on me. But I went over and shook Pete's hand. I tried not to remember his name was Pettis Perry, so I wouldn't crack up.

Harlem

There was no way that my mother and Pete could have survived if they had chosen to live in Bensonhurst. So they rented an apartment on the fringe of Harlem. Our building was on the corner of 138th Street and Amsterdam Avenue. From Number 501, on the top of the hill where we lived, 138th Street dropped precipitously toward the Hudson River. Downhill was mostly white. Just across Amsterdam Avenue, east of us, was the CCNY campus. Harlem stretched to the North, South, and East.

Our building, located in this no man's land between two hostile worlds, was a progressive outpost. Howard and Millicent Selsam lived above us. He was a Marxist philosopher and she wrote books for children, including one that I liked: *Play with Plants*. It was a practical introduction to genetics revealed through simple gardening experiments. An apartment several floors below was occupied by Betty Bacon, a librarian, who later became my mother's life-long friend. The rest of the neighbors ignored us in the usual New York manner. The building's ambiance was bohemian poverty mixed with the working class variety.

Our apartment, on the sixth floor, had a wonderful view. It was the only amenity; the rest of the place was a dump. The elevator rarely worked; the paint fell off the walls in clumps; the plumbing was archaic: we had a toilet that accepted feces on a platform just below the seat. When you pulled the chain that dangled from the water reservoir above your head, your excrement would be swept into a drain at the front of the toilet. My bed was near the bathroom and the stench from the rusty plumbing kept me awake at night.

Our TV had a wire coat hanger for an antenna that only brought in ghosts. I might have died of boredom if it weren't for the view. At night, from my west-facing bedroom window, I would stare across the Hudson at the amazing light show that Palisades Amusement Park put on to attract Manhattan visitors. During the day I would lean out a south facing window, with my legs folded up under me on a chair, and I would watch the people walking up and down the hill. In the morning large crowds would spill out of the IRT station on Broadway and proceed, in a clump, up the hill to the campus. Later in the day, people would trickle back the other way.

In the summer we kept the windows open and, on some nights, we could hear the outdoor concerts at Lewisohn Stadium, which was just across the street. I had heard classical music at my father's house: my Uncle Pat liked to play it on the radio, and no one in the Rizzo family seemed to mind. The tranquil sound of these stadium concerts reminded me of those Sundays in Brooklyn. The music would start at dusk and it would accompany the sight of the city beginning to light itself for the arrival of night.

Bensonhurst wasn't exactly a high-rise neighborhood so the experience of living up high was a new one for me. A lifelong battle with vertigo began soon after we moved there. Elevators were a new experience and they made me very uneasy. Ours was often out of order, and it always bounced ominously before coming to rest at any given floor. When the door opened, the distance between the landing and the elevator could vary by as much as a foot in either direction. Numerous re-paintings had been required; the layers of paint could be seen through the graffiti scratched into the walls. I learned the word *PUSSY* in that elevator. There were buttons for each of the seven floors and one for the basement. Pete had explained that we shouldn't go down to the basement alone, and that if the elevator started going below the ground floor we should push the emergency button. That would cancel everything and then we could push our floor.

When the elevator wasn't working, which was often, we took the stairs down to the lobby. You could exit the building, as you would from the elevator, through the front door, which opened from the outside with a key or by being buzzed in. This staircase also led up to the roof. It was possible to cross over from our roof to that of an adjoining building. You could exit down that building's stairs to Amsterdam Avenue.

I was always terrified when I was on the roof, in part because the open air enhanced my vertigo, but what really got my heart beating was not knowing who I would run into up there. Anyone lurking around on the roof was probably up to no good. Knowing that you could come down the fire escape from the roof to our bathroom window didn't help me sleep soundly. Our bathroom window was always locked but the thought that a thin piece of glass separated us from anyone who wanted to break in meant I always had an ear out for the tinkle of shattered glass.

It didn't take much imagination to see how vulnerable we were. While apartment buildings create the appearance of being like fortresses or castles, and in the more affluent buildings there is a doorman who guards the entry portal, in places like ours anyone could come and go almost at will. If the front door happened to be locked, which wasn't always the case, an intruder could gain access simply by coming in after one of our neighbors exited or entered. If enough buttons were pressed, sooner or later someone would buzz open the lock. Once you were in the building you had access to our roof, and to the other roof, and all the fire escapes.

Though we never had a break-in, or any close calls, I spent a lot of time thinking about the security of the apartment. These were real dangers, or so I thought, and plotting routes of ingress and egress kept at bay thoughts about other dangers that were more difficult to come to terms with. Occasionally I would slip into thinking about these other dangers.

At first, living way up in the air with my mother and this dark skinned man was so far from anything I had previously experienced that I didn't know what to make of it. Then, gradually, I began to understand the facts of my situation. Not long after we moved in I learned what a lynching was. I didn't think things like that happened in New York but who could tell what the future might bring? What if there was a race riot; what was I going to do? I could exit the building and blend in with white people but that meant leaving my mother, who would never abandon Pete. What if it was the other way around; what if I was the target that stood out? Could Pete protect us?

It wasn't just race riots that bothered me. I was beginning to see our situation through the eyes of the white people I had grown up with. We were freaks in their eyes: something so difficult to imagine, and so revolting, that just the sight of us was intolerable. I began to realize that strangers were looking away, and not seeming to notice us, when we were out in public. People who didn't avert their eyes were even worse; they would make no attempt to hide their hostility and disgust. It seemed to me that old ladies, in particular, were willing to make their feelings clear. They would single out my mother for their stares, and they were very aggressive about letting her know what they thought of her. She took it very well; I never saw her shirk their glances. She would stare right back at them as if *they* were being weird.

When we were around black people there was no looking away, and there was no hostility that I could detect. Later, I learned that some black women didn't take kindly to black men who were interested in white women. But I never observed any of that. The one thing I did notice was that Pete's standing seemed to be improved by being with us, particularly among black men. Black people seemed to notice him more than they would have if he happened to be walking alone. Black men would make eye contact with him.

Sundays at Grandpa Rizzo's

On some weekends I would go back to Bensonhurst to stay with Aunt Mary. Then, on Sunday afternoon, I would walk over to the Rizzos' for dinner. Everyone in my father's family would be there: Grandpa and Grandma Rizzo, my uncles Georgie and Patsy, Marie, my father's sister, her husband Sal, and my cousin Theresa. I was older than Theresa; I liked her and I think she liked me. Anyway, she always paid attention to me.

No one at my father's house, or at Aunt Mary's, or when I was with kids my age in Brooklyn, ever mentioned Pete. It was as though my life, when I wasn't in Bensonhurst, didn't exist. I was always aware of this and slightly anxious about it. On the playground when I heard the word *nigger* I would freeze. There would be a moment when I would consider whether I should say something. Then I would decide to let it pass, telling myself that confrontation was pointless. I wasn't going to change anything; making an issue of it would only call attention to me, and hold up the game. So I would let it pass. For a while I would feel small, intensely aware of what a coward I was. Luckily, I never had to deal with someone using the word at Aunt Mary's or my father's house. I don't know whether it was because they were more enlightened than the neighborhood kids or they were aware that it would bring up an issue no one wanted to mention.

As soon as I got to the Rizzos' I would go upstairs to Grandma and Grandpa's bedroom to pick up my allowance. Whenever I came over I would find four quarters in an eyeglass case in the top drawer of their night table. Sometimes, when I was left alone up there, I would go into the bedroom that my father shared with Georgie. In the top drawer of their dresser, on the right hand side, my father kept his watch-making tools rolled up in a polishing cloth. A tweezer, a magnifying eyepiece, and a small metal screwdriver that had smaller screwdrivers in its hollow handle were all in there. As far as I knew my father never used these tools.

But the object that really interested me in that drawer was on the left side. Wrapped in a small Nazi flag about the size of a Dodger pennant was a German Luger. Uncle Georgie had taken it from a German soldier he had captured. Georgie had been in the war like my dad, only Georgie had gone to Italy. He had always liked talking to the old men in the neighborhood, and he had learned the different dialects that they used, so they made him a translator for some General.

Georgie liked to joke around and tell stories but he never talked about the war. The only thing I knew for sure was that he had been wounded: he had a scar in the center of his palm to prove it. The story—I don't know how I heard it—was that a GI had gone crazy. He was about to shoot the General and Uncle Georgie had put up his hand to get him to stop. The GI shot Georgie and then my uncle wrestled the gun away from the guy.

Uncle Georgie was Italian through and through. It was just like him to try to stop the guy like that. There was no way he would have shot one of our own men, and that was why he ended up getting shot himself. When I thought about how the Italians had fared in the war, having to lick the Germans' boots and then being beaten by the Americans, I could see why people made jokes about Italians not liking to fight. Some people might think Uncle Georgie was a coward for not shooting the guy but to me he was just as brave as Graziano and Lamotta, and all the other Italians who had to prove how tough they were.

My fingers always trembled when I unraveled the Nazi flag. I was afraid of getting caught with the gun but that wasn't why I trembled. It had to do with the strangeness of that weird flag. The strong design of the swastika reminded me of the way the third rail pulls at you when you're standing on a subway platform. If you stare at it long enough, the swastika starts to blink on and off, like a neon sign. Even if there had been no such thing as Nazis, the swastika would be one powerful symbol you wouldn't want to fool around with.

As much as that flag bothered me, that feeling was nothing compared with the emotions caused by holding that gun. The Luger was heavy, so heavy I couldn't aim it straight ahead with one hand. From the weight, I knew there was a clip of bullets in the handle, but I wasn't sure how to get it out. Whenever I had the gun in my hand I felt powerful; I was equal to anyone else on the planet, as dangerous as any of the people who might harm me, and as safe as I would ever be.

One particular Sunday, when I was up there playing with the gun, the sound of someone starting up the stairs made my heart stop. Uncle Georgie shouted, "Richie, the spagetts are going to get cold."

"I'll be right down," I hollered, trying to make my voice sound like it was coming from Grandpa's bedroom.

I folded the gun up in the flag and put it back the way it had been. Then I tiptoed into Grandpa's bedroom, got my quarters, and went down to the dining room. Everyone was at the table; the big antipasto platter in the middle was already half empty. There was still plenty of prosciutto, salami (the thin hard one and the regular kind), provolone, mozzarella, caponata, the little wrinkled black olives and the green ones. All stuff I loved, the sharpest tastes. The pasta and the rest would be hard to resist but, if I didn't watch out, I could fill up on this stuff and not have room for later. My mouth was watering.

My place was next to my cousin Theresa. There was no way to get to my seat, without making people stand, so I hopped on the couch to get there. I knew I shouldn't be stepping on the couch with my shoes on but I figured they were all so busy stuffing themselves no one would notice. I tilted the chair back and slid in to my seat. Theresa gave me a smile to let me know I had done it gracefully. I was just beginning to feel like I had gotten away with it when Grandpa said, "Is that how you sit down?"

He made it sound like he was just asking for

information, but everyone knew better. He never asked a question just for the hell of it and he only spoke to kids when they had done something wrong. I had interrupted the meal and that made it a big deal. We all ate fast, without a lot of talking. I had been told to chew my food since I was a baby, but in my father's, and in Aunt Mary's house, no one ate slowly. And here was Grandpa having to take time out from eating to point out the error of my ways.

"Sorry, Grandpa," I said, and I was truly sorry that I had called attention to myself. Then Grandpa glanced at my father as if to say: *What more could I expect from a child of yours.* I felt sorry for my father and I felt terrible that I had brought this on him. I stared down at my plate. When I stole a glance at the other side of the table Uncle Georgie and Sal were looking down too, like there was a cockroach on their plates. Then Georgie said, "Richie needs some Pepsi."

It seemed like Georgie had said it to defy Grandpa, but I knew it was because he just couldn't stand to see a creature in pain. Grandpa didn't like what Georgie had done but he didn't say anything. Then Theresa bumped my knee under the table. Normally, I would have said *ouch* to embarrass her but this was no time to be joking around. Everything was going to be ok or she wouldn't have done that. Even though she was younger than me, she knew a lot more about how everything went at Grandpa's because she lived only a few houses away.

"What's the matter with the way he sits down?" It was Grandma. We all looked around at each other like it was a stupid question.

Marie answered, "When he went to sit, he stepped on the couch with his shoes."

"His shoes?" Grandma asked.

"His feet," my father explained. "To go sit down he climbed on the couch."

"Why did you climb on the couch with your shoes?" she asked.

"I couldn't get to my seat no other way. There was no room."

I was about to apologize again when Grandpa interrupted: "So instead of getting Arthur to move, like he knows he should do, he jumps up on the couch."

"Richie, you know you shouldn't climb up there with your shoes." Grandma's voice had no sharpness in it. She was giving me a way out.

"I know, Grandma. I won't do it no more."

I helped myself to some hard salami and provolone. Theresa passed me the bread. I could tell from the look she gave me it was all over.

Sal turned to my father and said, "A case of cigarettes fell off the truck. You need cigarettes?"

"What kind," my father asked.

"Luckys."

My father made himself sound disappointed. "I only smoke Camels."

Sal didn't give up. "Maybe some of your gumbas could use them."

Grandpa interrupted. "Arthur don't work for you."

I relaxed. Grandpa had zeroed in on another target. Sal had married his daughter, and as far as

Grandpa was concerned, nothing Sal could do would ever be good enough.

Sal was mad. "I know he don't work for me. I was just trying to do him a favor. He trades the Luckys for Camels. That's it, bing a bing, and he's got what he wants. I don't make nothing on the deal. What's wrong with that?"

Grandpa didn't give up: "You know what's wrong; when those Luckys show up on Eighteenth Avenue, they'll all know how they got there."

I felt sorry for Sal. He was just trying to do my father a favor. He liked to do things for us but Grandpa always acted like there was something wrong with him. He drove a truck and he hung out with a rough bunch of guys, but he really cared about us.

Uncle Georgie came back with my Pepsi. He handed me the bottle and went back into the kitchen. A minute later he came back with a steaming bowl of mostacelli that he put in front of Aunt Marie. I passed my plate to her. By the time she had put the pasta on it, Georgie was back with the sauce. Aunt Marie held my plate out and Georgie put some sauce on it. Usually at Aunt Mary's we mixed the sauce with the pasta before bringing it to the table. Here, at my father's, on Sunday anyway, each plate got its own sauce. That was the classy way to do it. The amazing thing was that the sauce in both houses tasted exactly the same. This was true even though my mother's family came from Catania, in Sicily, and my father's from Calabria, between the shin and the ankle.

We ate fast at most parts of the meal but I was

a speed demon when it came to pasta. It took me maybe two minutes, tops, to finish what was on my plate. I had no room for the braciola that was coming next. The problem was that if I asked to be excused, Grandpa would get mad again. He would want to know why I didn't save room for the main part of the meal. Since I had no choice, I started moaning.

"Mio, what's wrong?" Grandma asked.

"My stomach hurts, Grandma."

"You ate too fast," Grandpa said.

"I think I have to throw up," I said, and before anyone could speak, I stood up on my chair and went out the way I had come in. Over my shoulder I heard Grandpa say, "Again, with the shoes on the couch."

"I'll be okay. Nobody has to get up," I shouted as I flew upstairs. No one tried to follow me. I went into the bathroom, waited a few minutes; then I flushed the toilet. Then I came out and shouted down at them: "I'm feeling better. I'm going to lie down for a while."

When I was sure no one was coming up to check on me, I took out the Luger, stretched out on the bed, and pointed it up at the ceiling. It was easier to balance it this way. I squeezed the trigger lightly and made the hissing sound of a bullet going through the air. Downstairs I could hear an opera that Uncle Patsy was listening to on the radio. A lady was singing, *Un bel dì, vedremo.* I didn't know what the words meant but the way she held the notes, and the way the orchestra held them behind her, made me very sad.

"Everything okay up there?" It was Georgie's

voice. I told him I was feeling better and I would be right down. I wrapped the gun in the flag and put it back in the drawer. Something told me that Georgie had known what I was up to. If he did know it didn't matter; he wasn't going to say anything about it. He wouldn't want to get me in even more hot water with Grandpa. He and my father both knew that I knew about the gun being up there. My father had shown it to me in the first place. He liked to let me do things that he knew a kid would be dying to do. It was like taking me to the batting cage, or the bumper cars at Coney. What kid wouldn't have dropped dead to have a chance to handle a real gun? Of course he had told me it wasn't a toy, and I shouldn't play with it. Sure, that was like saying, *look but don't open your eyes.*

I knew I had better get going. If I stayed up here much longer either my father or Georgie was going to come up after me. They might be willing to give me the benefit of the doubt about not playing with the gun but they weren't going to let it go too far. I left the door to their bedroom open the way I had found it and headed downstairs to face Grandpa's music.

The Twins

It was going to be the first time I was out of the apartment on my own. My mother had given me a list of some groceries she needed from the small market on Amsterdam Avenue. The elevator decided to stop at the third floor on the way down. The doors opened, and then I couldn't get it to do anything else. So I took the stairs down the last three flights. When I came out of our building I saw two guys, twins, about my age, hanging out on the sidewalk between where I was and the corner. I made believe I hadn't noticed them and started walking toward Amsterdam Avenue as fast as I could. They didn't say anything as I passed but I heard their footsteps behind me as I walked up the hill. I had to keep myself from breaking into a run. Even if I made it to the grocery store, I would have to come back the same way and then they would be sure to start something.

I had made it to Amsterdam when one of them shouted, "Hey you."

I turned to face them. I had never seen twins that looked so much alike. The only visible difference between them, other than their clothing, was a harelip that one of them had. It occurred to me that what I was seeing might be genetically impossible.

"You live with that nigger, don't you?" the one with the harelip said.

It was the kind of question you couldn't

reasonably answer so I didn't say anything. I put a puzzled look on my face and turned to walk away. Then the lip pushed me. I wasn't expecting it; luckily, I kept my balance. Instead of running, which I had already rejected, I pushed back. Then the lip went into a boxing crouch. He was moving his fists around fast, and he looked as though he had done a lot of fighting. I was good at wrestling and I weighed more than him so I figured I would try to get in close.

When he feinted with his left and threw a roundhouse, I ducked inside the punch and grabbed him in a bear hug. I stuck my chin in his chest and bent him backwards to the sidewalk. I landed on top and dug my knees into his upper body. I knew my knees were hurting him and I waited for him to say, *I give*. I was about to ask if he'd had enough when a fist slammed into the side off my head. Then I felt a kick in my ribs and I keeled over, freeing the guy under me.

They were both standing over me. "I said, you live with that nigger," the lip shouted several times as he continued kicking me. I covered my head and pulled my knees up to my chest. They would wait a second or two between kicks. I knew this could go on forever if I didn't do something, so I screamed at the top of my lungs. That created enough of a diversion for me to get to my feet, and then I just started running as fast as I could. I kept going until I couldn't hear anyone behind me. Then I looked back and realized it was safe to slow down. I cut across the street and watched as they went back down the hill. Then I snuck back to my building.

When my mother opened the door, and saw that I hadn't bought the groceries, she got this puzzled look on her face. Then she got the picture. "Did they say something about Pete?"

It was going to be one hassle like this after another, and I wanted her to know how I felt so I said, "Why did we move here? I hate this place."

She told me they had originally talked about moving into central Harlem but that Pete felt it wouldn't be good for me to be the only white kid around. I had to hand it to her; she made it seem like it was all about what was good for me.

I suppose there is some good that comes out of every bad situation. That day was the beginning of an education in how to survive on the street. In the weeks and months that followed I learned how to check out a block for potential dangers; I discovered how to signal that you knew someone was trouble and that you were ready for it. Crossing the street or trying to ignore the problem usually wasn't a good option. The main thing was to establish that you were a non-victim. Sometimes it backfired, as in the *what are you looking at?* challenge. But even then there are options that can defuse the situation. I am always the first person around who notices when something is wrong on the street. This is not a great virtue but, then again, it isn't such a bad thing.

Big Pete

Thanks to the twins, and other real and imagined dangers, I was spending a lot of time indoors. That got me interested in reading in a big way. Neither Pete nor Rose was well educated. My mother had won an art scholarship to attend Hunter College but she hadn't attended because her family needed her income. Pete had started picking cotton at the age of ten; before that he hadn't had much schooling. He had taught himself to read, late in life, by starting on the *Communist Manifesto* and working his way up to *Das Kapital*. I didn't doubt either story. They were both really good at making sacrifices. Pete was meticulous when it came to sticking to a program. You could tell just by the way he read: with a pen or pencil in hand, underlining practically every word, slow, laborious, and ferociously determined.

For two people with little formal education they had an exceptionally large library. Reflecting their view of themselves as leaders in a movement that was going to transform the world, the collection leaned heavily toward history, particularly black history, and Marxism. At first, I was only interested in what little fiction there was. They had acquired quite a lot of Mark Twain. It was hard for me to understand how he got into their library. We never mentioned the N word in our home. It wasn't that I was told outright not to say it, it was just that we all knew who used it, and how it was used, and that made it way too heavy a word to be messing around with. The fact that someone in that house saw past Twain's use of the vernacular, to the thoroughly radical vision that was at the heart of his work, was completely out of sync with the one-dimensional perspective that dominated thought in that household. One of them got it, though, because I still own a complete set of Twain's works from their library. I'm really sorry that I never had the courage to ask about why his work was there; no doubt it would have led to an interesting conversation.

I quickly learned to refer to my stepfather as Big Pete. Everyone called him that. In part, this was to distinguish him from a younger white man named Pete who functioned as his secretary and bodyguard. Later the secretary was gone but a son had been born, and been given his father's name, so the nickname *Big Pete* remained. Big Pete wasn't very tall, so the name had more to do with conveying respect than anything else. There was a kind of logic in our world that was the exact opposite of the one operating in the rest of America. In our world, whites deferred to Negroes. It probably rubbed against the grain with most of the white people in our circle; I know it did with me. We believed in equality, so singling out one group for preferential treatment seemed disingenuous. But I never saw anyone, among the Communists and progressives we knew, violate this unspoken rule.

It wasn't just the unspoken rules of the milieu that made him Big Pete. He was a formidable, no-nonsense person. He was very literal-minded and his steel-trap mind was reinforced by a disposition that favored castigation. This was in step with the way discourse functioned in the Communist Party, and it was probably responsible for his becoming a Party leader. What mattered to me, though, was that I had a stepfather who was a major domo of the first order. I did my best to avoid his wrath. Though it's hard for me to admit it, the truth is he was very kind to me most of the time.

A boxing lesson

I attended PS 186 on 145th Street between Amsterdam and Broadway. Every day, from the time I left home for school, and then again after leaving school until I was back inside our apartment, I thought of only one thing: how I was going to manage to travel the seven and a half blocks safely. Most of the territory I had to pass through on the way home was controlled by one or another gang. Though a lone white boy on a Negro gang's turf wasn't much of a threat, I was the kind of toy someone might enjoy playing with. The white-controlled blocks were more of a problem. The white gang members would want to know which street I lived on, and since I wasn't up on which blocks were fighting with mine, I wouldn't know what to say. If I guessed wrong they would want to kick my ass, and if I guessed right they would want the name of someone I knew. They wouldn't believe that I didn't know anyone.

My usual strategy was to keep up a slow jog the whole way. One afternoon, after I arrived home out of breath as usual, Pete asked me to join him in the living room. He sat me down and told me he had noticed that I hadn't been bringing any books home from school. He wanted to know if I had a reason to be traveling light. He had guessed right; I had been leaving my books at school so that I could run when I needed to. Then he said he knew we lived in the kind of neighborhood where you had to be fast on your feet. I was too humiliated to explain about my fight with the twins so I just told him there were a lot of guys around looking for trouble.

I don't remember when I first heard the story. There was rumor going around among people close to our family that Pete might have killed a man. It was supposed to have happened in the South. Somewhere, I never heard where, a white deputy sheriff, or person in authority, was physically abusing a Negro man. Pete stepped in and he became the target of an attack, and in defending himself Pete had killed the man. That may have accounted for the fact that a great part of his adulthood was spent riding the rails; he crisscrossed the continent many times, and always avoided the deep South.

I do know one thing for sure: Pete was certainly capable of going to great extremes in defending what he believed in. So I wasn't too surprised when he explained to me that it was important for me to know how to take care of myself in violent situations. He told me he had learned a few things about fighting and that if I wanted he could show them to me. I didn't know what to say so I said nothing, and after a minute or two he went into a boxing crouch and started to teach me how to lead with my left. I didn't have the heart to tell him that nobody fought like that anymore: they used chains and knives and zip guns. A boxing crouch might get you a few laughs and that would be about it. He was doing his best to help me but it wasn't any use. Even though he might have killed some guy, there was no way he could begin to understand what it was like out on the street. But I went along with his lesson anyway. It ended with him holding up one of the bolsters from the couch and me throwing punches at it while I did my best to make my part of the charade look convincing.

PS 186

I didn't have to worry about keeping up in my new school. Back in Brooklyn we had already learned how to multiply fractions but here at PS 186 my class was just starting to learn what a fraction was. The thing that really worried me before I started—that I would run into the twins—wasn't going to be a problem: white kids didn't go to PS 186.

On the first day my mother packed a fried egg sandwich for my lunch. Every day after that, I would open my lunch bag hoping for something different. After the first week I told her I was tired of eggs but Pete liked eggs for breakfast. They were the only thing she kept in the refrigerator that had any chance of passing for lunch.

I took out the apple that was in the bag, and without bothering to open the wax paper to check the sandwich, I crumpled the bag like a snowball and made an easy two-pointer in the garbage can. Missing would have meant another try with the whole lunchroom watching. Probably I would have tried it behind my back, or maybe, if I happened to be feeling lucky, I would try a hook shot. But the pressure would be on: if I blew that shot, the whole lunchroom would have gone nuts.

Something like that could get you sent to the principal's office. They said you could get slapped in there. My mother told me that if any teacher ever touched me, I should tell her. I knew she would come to school and raise hell. Having a mother who came to school to yell at the teachers was just what every kid wanted. As usual, her solution would have been worse than the problem.

A lot of kids said they got whipped at home. I wasn't exactly sure what being whipped meant. The only whips I had seen were in movies. I had read about slavery but the idea of someone using an actual whip in a New York apartment seemed like a joke, except that none of the kids laughed when they said it.

As far as I could tell there were only two other white kids at my school. One was a boy. I talked to him a few times; he seemed nice enough. The other was a girl. At the time, I didn't know her at all. We met many years later. If you could call it a coincidence when two objects with similar, but very rare, trajectories intersect, then we met by coincidence. She had turned into a wonderful poet.

I was pretty sure that both these kids lived with white parents but I couldn't just go up to them and ask what they were doing at 186. I figured they were from progressive families. My mother used *progressive* to refer to people she agreed with. As far as I could tell being progressive meant you were against the way most things were done. There was no way anyone was more progressive than my mother.

The desks in our classroom were set up in rows: two desks next to one another and an aisle on each side. My desk partner was Henry. Henry was sweet: there was no other way to describe him. When he smiled he made you feel like he loved you. No one was afraid of him; even the girls knew he couldn't hurt a fly. Before I ran into Henry, I had never met anyone who liked everyone. At first, I couldn't believe it. Then, as I got to know him better, I could see that it was just the way he was.

When he saw I made my shot at the garbage can, Henry held his hand down low, with the palm up, so I could give him five. He had saved some shoe leather, and he peeled off a little strip for me and passed it under the table. Before coming here I had never tasted anything as sour as this apricot paste pressed on a sheet of waxed paper. They sold it in some of the small grocery stores near the school. Though I was addicted to shoe leather, I never had the money to buy it.

You had to be careful when you had something like that because there was always someone who would be after it. Henry knew how much I loved shoe leather; when he had it, he always saved some for me. From the way Henry treated me, I often felt like he loved me.

I never could figure out how he got his money. He wasn't the only kid like that; everyone at the school was poor, and the poorer you were, the more money you seemed to have for stuff like this. I was pretty sure some of the kids were stealing from home, but I didn't think Henry would do that.

We weren't supposed to leave the cafeteria without a pass. The teacher on duty was in the middle of getting some kids to clean up a big mess so Henry and I slipped out without being noticed. The lunchroom was noisy and crowded, and it was fun just wandering around the quiet halls. We headed downstairs. One staircase was for going up and separated from it by an iron grate was the other for going down. There were rules for everything at this school: a rule for where you could walk, one for how you walked, a rule for when you could talk, and a bunch of rules for when you couldn't talk. With the staircases set up like that, and the oldness of the place, and all the rules, it felt like you were in jail.

So, of course, the only thing you ever thought about was how to get away with breaking the rules. As soon as a teacher turned her back it would start: people would throw things, pass notes, and generally act up. There was so much of it going on the teachers couldn't keep track of it all. Most of them looked the other way on purpose. But a few kept an eagle eye out and spent all their time catching kids who were out of line.

Someone was walking down our staircase ahead of us. I could tell by the perfume it was Mrs. Washington, the teacher from across the hall. She seemed like a nice lady; she wasn't always scowling like our teacher. Still, I didn't want to be caught by her. We waited to let her get further ahead; after we heard her open the door to leave the staircase, Henry ran his hand across his forehead like he was wiping off sweat, and I cracked up. Then we continued on down.

When we came out on the first floor the hall was empty. We couldn't keep going on like this;

sooner or later we would be caught. There was a boy's bathroom down at the end of the hall. I was about to tell Henry we should hide in the bathroom when I realized he was already on his way there. Just before we reached the bathroom door, I heard the click of a woman's heels coming down the hall just around the corner from where we were. Henry pushed the door open and started to go in. He stopped in his tracks, and because he was blocking me, I pushed him inside.

Then I saw why he had frozen. There was a ceiling pipe that ran across the stalls. Hanging from that pipe was a kid. I had seen him a few times during recess, but we had never spoken. On assembly days the boys were supposed to wear ties. Today wasn't an assembly day but he had on a tie. His belt was draped over the pipe with his tie knotted into it. His head was over to one side and the rest of his body was leaning back the other way. He wasn't moving.

It might have been a joke. If it was, Henry had fallen for it. He was as scared as I was. Neither of us spoke. We both concentrated on the footsteps outside in the hall. The woman slowed as she came to our door as though she knew something was wrong. I could almost feel her, on the other side of the door, asking herself if she should check out our bathroom. Finally, her footsteps started up again and she continued down the hall.

The kid's eyes were open but they weren't focused on anything. I thought he might be smiling a little and that made me think Henry had planned this. Then it really hit me that he was dead and we were in big trouble. Just being in the same room with him made me shiver; I knew that as long as I didn't touch him nothing could happen to me but I couldn't help feeling that something invisible—some germ or bad air—could come out of him and infect me.

I could see how he had done it. He stood on top of the flusher and balanced himself long enough to knot his tie into the belt. Once that was done he jumped off. Imagining the rest was horrible: he didn't fall far enough to break his neck so he probably kicked around while he was choking. Maybe he tried to save himself. It was only natural that, sooner or later, your body would try to get air. What if he changed his mind and couldn't get back up? Once you jumped off the flusher it would be almost impossible to get your feet back up behind you long enough to unhook the tie. I could see him kicking, maybe grabbing the belt and trying to pull himself up, not having enough strength to continue, and then going unconscious.

I whispered, "Did you know him?"

Henry nodded and said, "His whole family is gone. His mother and his brother both; they did the same. She put her head in the oven and, a couple of days later, the brother jumped off the roof." Then Henry went to the door and opened it a crack. He said, "That teacher's gone; let's make it."

We slipped out into the hall and flew back upstairs to the cafeteria. No one seemed to notice us as we sat down in a corner by ourselves.

"What if he wasn't dead?"

Henry sounded as if he had just thought of it.

After we had started running the thought had crossed my mind. But there was no way I was going to stop and go back to find out. I answered, trying to make myself sound like I believed it. "There was no way he wasn't dead."

Henry didn't say anything for a while. I could tell he was trying to make up his mind whether to believe me. Finally he said, "Put it out of your mind."

I knew exactly what he meant. I remembered the time I thought I could see into the future and how, eventually, I was able to forget it. Later on, you might remember how weird it was, but each time you came back to it, it would bother you a little less. Even though this thing wasn't completely over yet, I was already starting to push it out of my mind. As long as nothing else happened I figured I would be okay. The trouble was, for a while at least, whenever I would see Henry, I would have to think about it. "Let's never talk about it," I said.

"Talk about what?"

To let him know we were on the same wavelength I asked him why he had money for shoe-leather all the time. He told me his mother gave him the money. I was pretty sure he wasn't going to jive me after all that had just happened. But the block Henry lived on was one of the most run-down blocks in the whole run-down PS 186 neighborhood. How someone poor enough to live around here could afford to give her kid money all the time, especially when he wasn't her only child, was something I couldn't figure out. But this was a question I could not ask, so instead I told him I thought he was lucky.

The bell rang, and we went back to our room. Then the sirens started and they kept getting louder and louder until they stopped on our street. I caught Henry's eye and looked away quickly so no one would notice the look that passed between us. Nothing out of the ordinary happened after that. By the time the teacher let us out for the day everyone in the school was talking about it.

A Brooklyn Weekend

We had already won two games when Abe showed up. My partner was this fat kid who wore black-ball gloves even though we were playing with a Spaulding. It was point-game. I served long to the worst guy's left. He had backed up as I started the serve so, instead of having to take it on a short hop, the way I had planned, he let it bounce high and then he hit it with his right. His arm had a lot of swing behind it.

I knew our time was about up. My partner's tee shirt was drenched and his face was red. I tightened my stomach and made myself move forward as the ball whizzed past my ear. If the ball made it to the wall it would be low. The thing I love about sports is the way you can sense where a ball is going to be from just a glimpse of its arc. My only problem was getting there in time. When it hit the wall I was already reaching in front of me, my finger tips scraping the ground. I brought my hand up as it bounced, got a piece of it, and sent it low toward the wall. Then I fell flat on my chest. Everyone hollered when it made the wall; it was a perfect killer. My partner reached down and gave me his hand. As he pulled me up he said, "That's it for me."

Abe had been watching the game; when I looked over at him he said, "Great shot." I thanked him, and as we started walking away he asked, "So what's it like in New York?"

Whenever I came to stay with Aunt Mary on weekends I acted as though I was still living on Sixty-eighth. I hadn't told him, or anyone else in the neighborhood, anything about my life in Manhattan. I usually hung out in the park all day going from one sport to another until I was exhausted. I didn't know most of the guys in the park. Other than a nod or two, we didn't talk much. If we did have a conversation it was always about sports.

"It's not much different from here, bigger buildings is all." I figured this would give him the idea that I was now living in a fancier neighborhood. As far as Abe and my other friends in Bensonhurst were concerned, Manhattan was a place where rich people lived. They all had heard of the Harlem slums, but I didn't think they would connect me with that. After all, we could have stayed at Aunt Mary's; why would we want to live in a slum?

"Is school harder there?"

"Yeah, you have to wear a tie all the time like in Catholic School—not just for assemblies." It wasn't that I liked lying; it was just that I couldn't tell the truth. If I did he would think I was some kind of freak. My story had to be realistic; if the school was fancier I guessed they would probably wear ties.

"I have a cousin that goes to Dalton. Have you heard of it?"

He was testing me. I never should have started this bullshit story. I asked if he wanted to play basketball. There was an open court, but I didn't have anything to leave for a ball deposit. Usually the guys who were willing to be responsible for the ball were the worst players, and when they lost they would want to take the ball with them. We found a young kid and got him to leave his keys, and when we chose sides, we dumped him. I felt sorry for him but the truth was if we had picked him we would have lost. Abe was shorter than me and you had to have at least one tall guy on a three-man team.

We played a couple of games and then we lost. I was ready to go home and so was Abe. On the way out he asked if I had heard about what had happened to a neighbor, a man who drove a bus like my father. I shook my head. He said, "Everyone knew he got all that crap in his garage by stopping the bus and picking up junk that he saw in the street. What no one knew, but my father read about in the paper, was that every day for twenty-five years he would finish off his coffee in the morning and then fill up his big thermos with motor oil. Once he had saved up a few gallons, he would sell it. They got him for grand larceny: over the years he stole thousands of dollars worth of oil."

It didn't surprise me that he had taken the oil. What surprised me was that he had sold it. I had never known him to let go of even the worst piece of junk that he found. I felt sorry for him: the way I saw it, you shouldn't steal from friends or people who couldn't afford it. My mother was always pointing out how rich people stole big time with nothing but a pen, and she said they never got caught, so I figured it wasn't wrong for some poor sucker to take something no one was going to miss.

Abe told me his father had said the bus

driver's son's college expenses had probably come out of that oil. As much as I felt sorry for the old man, I felt sorrier for the son. The son probably figured the cost of his schooling had pushed his father into stealing. It was a relief knowing you weren't the only one in a tight spot because of your parents. They hadn't started out to mess up our lives, but they had screwed things up so nicely that we would have to spend the rest of our lives trying to straighten out the mess they made.

Abe's next remark shook me. "No one knows why you moved to New York."

Once my heart had stopped thumping, I tried to guess if he knew anything. I wanted to tell him, and at the same time I was scared to death he would find out. He was a good guy and probably the only person in Bensonhurst I could talk to. For Abe it must have seemed like I had stepped into the fifth dimension: he knew I existed when I was away from Brooklyn, but he had no idea what went on wherever I had gone. He had to be curious. I figured he probably wouldn't have asked in that way if he had a clue about what was really going on. He couldn't have made his question seem so normal.

The problem was there was also no way I could begin to talk about Pete. I couldn't say my mother married a nigger, which is the word most people in Bensonhurst would have used. I would have said *colored guy*, or something like that. And the words were the easiest part. I couldn't just tell him I thought Negroes were okay. He would have to be around them, the way I was, before he could even begin to understand. He would have to get to know someone like Henry and then, maybe after that, I could tell him. Otherwise it was going to be one question on top of the next, and it would end up with my mother in bed with Pete.

I knew there was nothing I could say that would allow him to hide how horrible he thought the whole thing was. Then I would have to start defending myself, and my mother. That was something I wouldn't do. I might stand up to Abe and tell him I was proud of what my mother had done. Maybe I could say that to the other kids, which I would eventually have to do because Abe would tell his brother, and that would be that. Sooner or later, I would start back-pedaling; I would end up saying: *it's not that bad,* or, *don't blame me for what she did.*

If it ever got to that point I might as well be dead. They would be all over me and I would feel terrible. At least this way I was anonymous. All I really wanted was to be able to come to Brooklyn for a little rest and relaxation without having to stand out. I just wanted to be another kid in the park. I couldn't blame Abe; he was just trying to be my friend. It was just that I had no choice; so I lied. "My mother got a job in New York."

We had reached Aunt Mary's. Abe asked if I was going to be around next weekend and I told him that I wanted to come but I wasn't sure if I could. Then I went inside to get ready for my father to pick me up and take me back to Manhattan. He always stayed out in the car, and I didn't want him to have to sit out there while I got ready. I threw my stuff into my canvas bag. I gave Aunt Mary a kiss. She had these pop out eyes that were always watery, but just now they were especially watery. Then I gave Grandpa a hug. He usually went a few days between shaves. No matter how much I tried to stay away from his cheek, he always managed to rub his scratchy beard up against me. Although he was old, Grandpa was still as solid as all the stone and cement he had worked with.

"You come again next week." Though he had said it like it was an order, I knew it was really a question. He wanted me to say *yes* even though he knew I didn't have control of when I came. When I didn't reply he gave me a look that told me he wasn't happy with nothing for an answer. "You come," he said as if I knew, not from his words, what he was saying. The thing was I did know. A lot of people thought he was stupid because they didn't understand his way of communicating. If you halfway tried you would always figure out what he was getting at.

By the time I got outside my father was waiting. I wasn't surprised that he hadn't blown the horn. He wouldn't have wanted to call that much attention to himself. When I opened the car door I held my breath. There was a smell in the car that I always tried to get used to gradually. It was from the cigarettes my old man had smoked in there. The smell wasn't the same as fresh smoke, which wasn't too bad; it was the smell of smoke that had settled and gone sour, just like the smell of a dead person would be different from how they smelled when they were alive.

My father asked if I wanted to play the radio. Instead of answering, I turned it on. If I had been alone I would have listened to music but I knew the ball game was what he would want. Baseball on the radio was for people who wanted to hear the same thing over and over. You were supposed to think the announcer was repeating the count for people who couldn't follow the game, or had just tuned in, but really it was for people like my father who loved hearing the same old count over and over: balls, strikes, outs, runs, and men on.

I made myself listen to it like it was music. The announcer had this soft voice, a smooth, relaxing sound over the short barks of the fans. In the whole world there was no other sound like this. It could calm you down even though it was actually really one man talking over thousands of people shouting. The other thing about the game on the radio was that you always had something you could talk about.

Then, over everything else, I heard the sharp crack of the bat. Mel Allen's only words were, "It's deep." You could tell by the way he said it that it was gone. You were supposed to still have hope—an announcer couldn't put the cap on it until it actually happened—but you knew from his voice the ball was out of the park. There was a short silence; everyone in the park was taking in a breath, then a lot of screaming. My father didn't show any sign that something terrible had just happened. Finally he said, "He should have been in the showers two innings ago."

He must have been listening to the game before he picked me up. Maybe he had turned it off so I could choose whatever I wanted to hear. It wasn't that he didn't like the pitcher, or the coaching, this was just his way of dealing with setbacks: you take it out on your own side.

"They never should have started with a southpaw in the first place," I said.

This seemed to satisfy my father. We were just going into the Brooklyn Battery Tunnel. I hadn't been paying attention to the road. Usually I prepared myself for the tunnel. Now, I closed my eyes and tried to control my breathing. This was the longest underwater tunnel in the world and if one of the walls ever cracked you wouldn't have much of a chance.

I looked over at my father. You could tell from the way he held the wheel what a great driver he was. He kept his hands down, almost in his lap, and he gripped the wheel with two fingers of each hand, the way bus drivers did. He didn't have much of a build but there was no belly hanging over his belt like a lot of guys his age had. On the pinkie of his left hand he wore a small gold ring. It was flat on top with a black stone and a little diamond set in the center of the stone. He could have used a shave.

He made his move to the lane on his left and he sped up a little. We slid in between the Oldsmobile, which was ahead of us, and a car coming up on the left. My father had timed the move just right. The guy coming up didn't have to hit the brakes, and once we passed the Oldsmobile we moved back so the guy behind could pass. The smooth way he had done that relaxed me, and by the time we were out in the open air I was sorry the tunnel was over.

We headed up the Westside Highway, and it wasn't long before I saw the Queen. There were two sister ships: The Queen Mary and The Queen Elizabeth. The Elizabeth, which was coming up on our left, was the largest passenger ship in existence. I asked my father to slow down so we could get a good look, and he said he would do the best he could. Before I knew it she was slipping past us. The name was written on the prow, just where I knew it would be. The aircraft carrier Missouri was supposed to be bigger, but seeing the Elizabeth, up close like that, I couldn't believe it.

"When you were in the navy did you ever go on anything like that?"

"Naw, I was on some troop ships but nothing near to being that big."

"Did you ever see anyone get shot?"

"No, I told you; we were in the middle of nowhere. There was no fighting anywhere near where we were. We were just there to occupy the island. We had a big radio antenna and our radiomen were supposed to listen to the ships and planes, ours and theirs. They never even got close to us."

"So you didn't see any corpses or anything?"

"Corpses? Nope; I'm telling you, there was nothing but coconut trees out there. No people, no animals, just a few trees and a lot of sand."

"So you've never seen a dead person?"

I knew, as soon as I said it, that I had gone too

far. My father never took his eyes off the road; but, right then, he turned and stared at me.

"Why are you so interested in corpses?"

I hadn't started out to tell him about the kid who hung himself but, for a second, I almost let it out. Then I realized that if I did tell him, he would have blamed my mother. It wasn't like he would have done anything. Aunt Mary might have tried to do something but not him. Still, even though probably nothing would have come of it, I couldn't let my mother down. All I could do was wish I could have told him.

I was starting to feel like I always did on Sundays when he drove me home. I hated going back to Manhattan. In Brooklyn, as tense as it could get, I never had a problem relaxing. It was just sports morning till night. It was easy to blend in, and everyone I knew had his life under control. All my relatives knew people. They had all gone to school together and hung out together since they were kids. Here in Manhattan the only people we knew were Pete's comrades. It's true these comrades, as they called one another, acted like they cared about us, and they tried to help out, but it wasn't like you had known them all your life. Bensonhurst was safe. Here I had to spend a lot of my time worrying about what was going to happen next. Guys would go after you for no reason at all, and they wouldn't be fooling around. No one knew anyone else so there was nothing to hold someone back. The tears were streaming down my cheeks. I didn't want my father to know so I made believe I was looking out at

Harlem, and I used my sleeve to dry my eyes.

Uncle Patsy

It seemed to me that my uncle Patsy was almost as out of place in Bensonhurst as I was. Like my grandfather, Patsy was an optometrist. He served a term as president of the Amateur Astronomers Association of New York. He read widely, loved the poetry of Walt Whitman, and was an avid classical music fan. It was a mystery to me how Patsy managed to be who he was.

Here is what I know. My grandfather Achilles, arriving in America at age eleven from the small village in Italy, somehow managed to learn to speak English without an accent. He completed enough education to start an optometry business. His store was located near Columbia University. Of Achilles' three sons, only my uncle Patsy was college educated.

Though Patsy, with his greater awareness of the wider world, should have been able to find a way to communicate with me, he never made an attempt to discuss my situation. I believe his reticence was related to his marginality. There were few supports, in this insular Italian community, for a life of the mind. He was viewed, perhaps occasionally with admiration, as an eccentric. In everyone's eyes, including those of his family, Patsy was not a person one could easily understand or identify with. He survived by turning inward; he was civil to everyone, and at the same time he remained aloof from everything around him. Any disruption of the routine he had established, any open confrontation with community norms, threatened to bring the entire project of his life crashing down.

He had his books, his music, and his astronomy. That amounted to an almost sufficient life; he wasn't about to go mucking around in politics or social advancement. Though I was a person with one foot in a wider and more interesting world I think he knew that opening up to me would have made his own place in this tight-knit community problematic. This—and the complications that would have arisen from meddling in his brother's life—explained why we never made meaningful contact with one another. Had we done so, I am certain both our lives would have been greatly enhanced.

I was aware, soon after leaving Bensonhurst, that I was on a trajectory similar to the one my uncle Patsy had taken. While he had become a self-centered outsider in order to be able to appreciate the things he loved that wasn't what was driving me. If you told me I was a budding intellectual I would have laughed. I suppose you could say I valued my life, in the literal sense, and that was what I was protecting. But that would be a very base way of coming to terms with my increasing self-absorption.

No doubt fear was a big part of it. I was afraid of the twins and the gangs. Real or imagined, these visceral fears (thoughts of being beaten or killed) were enough to keep me indoors. But I wasn't completely anti-social; in school I felt somewhat safe and I got along fine with the other kids. I was increasingly turning inward for another reason. The world around me had abruptly become a place that was incomprehensible. I needed a time out in order to clear up who I was and what my place in all this was.

Going underground was a way of accomplishing this; I cut off access to my inner world so that I could come to terms with the absurdity of what I was seeing. There were some things that were very clear: I was living in a country where people constructed intense hatreds based on what I now knew were superficial characteristics. I very badly needed to understand how that could be. If I could understand that I might be able to survive.

Though I tried to cope with daily life I knew I didn't belong in this, or perhaps any other, social milieu. It is possible that everyone feels this way; I don't know about that. I do know I was extremely alienated. I had a very strong sense that I was a spy, not for any group or nation, I was a spy whose only mission was to remain invisible. If uncle Patsy could remain an island unto himself in Bensonhurst I could do it in Manhattan.

Paul Robeson

Pete and Rose tried not to show how excited they were, but the surge in energy was obvious, more so in my mother's case than Pete's, but even Pete, usually unflappable, couldn't hide his delight. So I wasn't surprised when they announced that Paul Robeson was on his way up. It may have been that his visits weren't frequent, and yet they were so intimate, that accounted for the fact that the three of us were uniquely in accord on the significance of the event.

I wondered what it must have been like for Paul to get so much adoration in encounters like this. Not everyone admired him: there were plenty of people who hated him, a few who had probably considered murdering him. Maybe that was why we loved him so much; he was fearless while remaining gentle and kind. It wasn't good for anyone to be revered in this way; it had to warp your perceptions. But none of us, including Paul, could change the way we felt.

Living with Pettis Perry, I had already acquired a good deal of experience with grandiosity. My mother, and most of Pete's comrades, dealt with him as if he had some hereditary right to special treatment. Politics probably fueled it, but it was expected that you would defer to him on just about everything. Leaving aside what that meant for the rest of us, I knew this was not good for Pete. Once something like that gets going, though, it's very difficult to break out of it.

If Paul was affected by the adulation, it certainly wasn't apparent on the surface. I had never met anyone who focused so intently on me. Even though I knew he had created this same rapport with everyone in the room, he still made me feel special. His smile was contagious; it just opened out and grabbed you. To say that we were all in love with him might be an exaggeration, but in these moments of personal contact it wasn't far from the truth.

I didn't mind that he would bounce me, as grown up as I was, on his knee. He would make a joke of it and then he would tell some interesting story. This would go on for a while and then my mother would signal that it was time to leave the two men alone in the living room. Though I always wanted to hang around I knew Paul hadn't come over to play with me, or shoot the breeze with our family; he was there to meet with Pete.

Paul was very close to the Party. Whether or not he was an actual member only mattered to people who were unfamiliar with Party life. It was true that actual card-carrying Party members were less free to make independent decisions. When you joined you committed to a process called Democratic Centralism. Basically this meant that, once the leadership had decided on a course, you either followed the line or you quit. The polarization of U.S.—Soviet relations was already well under way, and the flip-flops required of the U.S. Party by the Soviets had taken its toll on the Party's membership.

Because he had an international reputation

Paul was relatively free of Party discipline. He could have argued for almost any view, including remaining silent on major issues, and the Party wouldn't have publicly objected. But for Paul the commitment wasn't to a Party; it was to a socialist world-view that sought to put inequality in America—and in the rest of the world—at the top of any political agenda. The fact that he didn't abandon this view meant that he had come under blistering attack for his internationalist and anti-imperialist statements.

The Party leadership was concerned that he was being pushed to the periphery and isolated, especially with regard to mainstream Negro life. The truth was that as an artist, and as a political figure, Paul's contacts were overwhelmingly with white people. Jackie Robinson, usually not outspoken on political matters, had publicly disagreed with a statement that Paul was alleged to have made about Negroes not being willing to participate in a war against the Soviet Union. (Paul's actual statement, I believe, was more ambiguous than the widely reported version appearing in the press at the time.)

These meetings with Pete were about how Paul could strengthen his ties in the Negro community. Pete urged him to spend more time in Harlem and to increase his profile at his brother's church. Paul's brother was the pastor of a major congregation in Harlem, and Paul was always welcome there. Pete always emphasized how important the church was as a force in the Negro community. In Paul's case it could be, and was, a source of sanctuary and support in difficult times.

This strategy was somewhat successful, but it couldn't reverse the political direction that the country was taking. The left was being forced into a defensive posture that would make it increasingly irrelevant as the fifties unfolded. Paul and Pete, two black leaders whose words might have carried weight when the civil rights movement exploded in the sixties, had already by that time been effectively silenced.

Paul had been scheduled to sing in Peekskill in late 1949 and that concert provoked a violent response from right wing racists. People were attacked, and Paul's life was in danger. When the House of Representatives debated the Peekskill events, the Representative from Mississippi shouted that the American people were not in sympathy, "with that Nigger Communist and that bunch of Reds who went up there."

If Paul was intimidated by any of this it was not apparent when he came to visit us. He always seemed at ease. At the time I had no inkling that the pressures he faced were taking their toll. The waning years of his life were very difficult for him; he was hospitalized and given shock therapy for depression. Had I not been lucky enough to meet Paul, the story of his life would have seemed to me to be a myth embellished in the way myths are. But the fact was this larger-than-life figure actually existed. I was lucky to get to know him and to learn first-hand just how far the human potential could extend.

The Arrest 1951

After she opened the door to my bedroom, my mother just stood there staring at me like she was in shock. She was pregnant, and I thought she might be going into labor.

"Get dressed. Pete is going to be arrested. They're arresting the whole Party leadership."

It took some time for the meaning of that to sink in. Once I got it, fear set in. I had heard enough about German concentration camps to ask myself where the line would be drawn: Communists, friends of Communists, families? It wasn't clear how she knew they were coming. The cops didn't send out invitations before they grabbed someone. I started to relax; it was probably just one of her crazy paranoid ideas.

The sun had already come up, but I knew it was really early. Then there was a loud knock at the front door. It didn't sound friendly. I didn't know what to do. Part of me didn't want to be there. Another part of me said I should at least go and say goodbye. I slipped on my dungarees and stood in the hall just outside my room.

My mother said, "Who is it?

An angry voice said, "FBI, open up."

I had figured it would be the regular cops. This meant it was a much bigger deal than I thought. The idea that these super professional FBI agents were about to come into our house, and treat us like freaks, made me want to hide in my room. I wondered if they would have their guns drawn, and it occurred to me that they might start shooting. I decided to stay put and duck into my room if that happened. My mother opened the door and then she started screaming. It wasn't a leave-us-alone scream; this was the kind of scream you would let out if someone had stuck you with a knife.

Even though the cops hadn't touched her, she was screaming to beat the band. As far as I could see, no one was doing anything. She seemed to be trying to attract as much attention as she could. Then she started shouting, "Rape." That was when one of the FBI cops stepped through the door. He was wearing a fedora and a regular topcoat, no badge or anything, but you knew he was a cop. He had this disgusted look on his face, like he was cleaning a dirty toilet. He ignored my mother. Pete was putting on his coat in the living room, and the cop pointed at him and made a motion to let Pete know that he was supposed to come outside. Then the cop backed out on the landing by the elevator again.

Though the FBI agent was acting like he was in charge, it was obvious my mother had made him very nervous. These guys had just come here doing their job and she was turning it into a three-ring circus, playing the victim to the hilt. It didn't make any difference that it wasn't going to do any good, Pete was going with them no matter what; still she had to show them she had it in her to make life difficult for them.

Pete finally got his coat on and went to the door. He was taking his good time about it, showing them that he also wasn't a pushover. The two of them were fighting back the only way they could. They were being brave; but the whole thing was dumb. None of what they were doing would make a difference. It was like they were in a factory on an assembly belt and someone had turned on the juice. Pete would be handed along from one cop to another until he was sitting in a cell down at West Street. Nothing he or my mother did was going to affect that.

When Pete reached the front door my mother shut up. He kissed her, and then he looked down the hall at me. I think he was expecting me to come up and give him a hug. I kind of waved from where I was. I know that was the wrong thing to do, but it was the best I could muster. There was no way I wanted those cops paying attention to me. Pete waved back. It seemed to me that he understood how I was feeling because he gave me a little smile that said it was okay. Then he went through the door, and my mother followed him out.

She must have ridden down in the elevator with them because, when I went to the window and looked out, she came out with them on the sidewalk. There was an unmarked Ford double-parked out in front. Pete had his hands behind his back. I couldn't see the handcuffs, but I knew they were on him. My mother stood by the curb and watched as they put him in the back seat. Then one of the cops went around and got in the back with him. The other guy got behind the wheel and took off. My mother stood down there a long time after they had gone.

My Brothers

My brothers were born about a year apart. Little Pete was first; his full name is Pettis Dennis Perry (the middle name for Eugene Dennis, leader of the Communist Party). Then Fred was born; his full name is Frederick Douglass Perry.

Naming a child is usually an expression of hope, an attempt to locate the child in an imagined future. Even names that don't have easily identified referents often provide a clue of what the parent was thinking. My first and middle names for example: Arthur and Richard hint at my mother's aspirations. Anglo Saxon names clearly do not belong with Rizzo. Rose obviously wanted to avoid any identification of me with the provincial world into which I was born. In fact, when I asked my mother why she named me Richard she replied that she had chosen Richard because it was the name of the hero, Richard Hannay, in John Buchan's spy novels. No one who knew me used my first name, which was my father's name. The hopes embodied in the names chosen for my brothers are about as transparent as they could have been. That Big Pete and Rose could have hoped for an apolitical future for their children would have been unthinkable.

Though *half brother* is the commonly used term for our familial relationship, as far as I know, Pete and Fred never referred to me in that way. I am sure I have never used that term for them. *Half brother* is too close to *half breed*, a word used by people who think in terms of "pure" breeding. We always use brother. Often, when they introduce me, or I them, we experience a slight delight in saying, *this is my brother*. We never offer an explanation and we never get a request for one.

Throughout their early childhood, I spent a lot of time with them. When they were tiny I cuddled them; later I changed diapers, sang to them, and appointed myself to the general role of doting older sibling. Though my behavior garnered a good deal of adult adulation, I did it because I truly enjoyed caring for them.

Unfortunately not all my emotions were positive. I also resented them, not so much for supplanting me; what I couldn't tolerate was their extreme self-centeredness. I was too immature to understand that these two boys were focused on their own needs the way all children their age were. Little Pete, in particular, brought out the sadist in me. He was very energetic and determined, and I would block his efforts in a way that tortured him.

I hid the sadistic aspects of our relationship from the adults as best I could. I don't think my mother or Pete knew what was going on. I was never cautioned about it. I'm not sure whether any of my actions did any permanent damage. I don't think so; it was certainly not any more pain than is usually inflicted on younger siblings by their older brothers or sisters. No physical harm ever came of it. Yet the guilt I felt, especially later in life, was fairly strong.

As always, part of my guilt had to do with race.

My behavior toward my brothers reflected, in a minor way, the treatment that black people usually received at the hands of whites. I am almost certain it was the fact that I was older, not race, that produced my desire to lord it over them. But of course there is no way of establishing the truth of the matter. Clearly my brothers were innocent: no matter how much their demanding behavior annoyed me, on some level I must have known that they were just doing what kids normally did. Luckily, they weren't completely powerless; like all kids, they knew how to call attention to their suffering. My awareness of this probably kept worse things from happening.

What is most interesting about the way I dealt with my brothers, and the resulting guilt I felt, was the fact that, for all my strong feelings of kinship, I defined them as racially different from me. At no time did I ever consider them white. I had heard the term *mulatto* but I never used it because it had what I believed to be a pejorative connotation. I didn't know then that the term probably derived from the Spanish word for mule (a neutered creature having been created by crossing a horse with a donkey).

Since the term *mixed race* was not in common use at the time I didn't have an accurate way of describing my brothers. But even if I had known of such a term I would have thought of them as black. This was the way almost everyone, black and white, thought in those days. It was well known that there were resentments in the black community that derived from how dark a person's skin was. In general, lighter skinned Negroes were ascribed higher status. But the story doesn't end there: status is malleable and certainly many darker skinned people had a different view of the hierarchy.

The other interesting thing with regard to how I thought about my brothers' race was that I never felt that any of the qualities that I associated with them had been produced by their race. I knew, of course, that from very early on race played an important role in how they were perceived and in how they viewed the world. But the idea that they had any particular personality trait, any ability, or disability because they were black never once occurred to me. This seemed so obvious to me, having lived with them from their birth, that it was very difficult for me to understand how anyone could see it any other way.

Taps

It wasn't as though someone had to tell me our apartment was bugged; everyone, including the people who came over for meetings, communicated in very strange ways. Sometimes Pete would be in the middle of a conversation and he would stop, grab a notepad, write something down, and show it to the person he had been talking to. With stuff like that going on, it didn't take me long to figure out what was happening.

Writing was the most precise way we indicated something without saying it. We had other ways as well: I might be talking about someone; instead of saying his name I would use a description: *the guy who sails* or *the one with two girlfriends*. After a while this way of talking just came naturally.

Not only did I learn to communicate this way, I began to think this way as well. I never made a conscious effort to forget names but I certainly didn't try to remember them. Since I wasn't expected to come up with a name in conversation, there was no need to make an effort to learn them. Much later in life I was able to do exceptionally well with the names of obscure theorists that I was studying but I couldn't, for the life of me, remember the names of my fellow classmates.

I wasn't sure if every conversation in the house was recorded. Some of the fear of explicit conversation that dominated our household may have been paranoia. But it was pretty clear that something was going on. Not long after Pete was arrested a small group of Party leaders, who were out on bail, skipped town. The FBI was searching for them. From time to time, I was aware that I was being followed. If they were following me, it seemed likely they were bugging the phone and probably the house as well.

Knowing that your most intimate sounds are constantly being monitored is extremely stressful. Once I realized we were bugged, a desire to be soundless began to augment my habitual wish for invisibility. I was angry at the violation of our privacy but there was nothing I could do about it. Instead, when I was home alone, I would walk around the house shouting obscenities and directing them at the FBI agents so they wouldn't think I was crazy. Occasionally I would have conversations with them that, of necessity, took the form of a monologue.

People who are exposed to severe ill treatment (rape, torture, or other abuse) frequently live the rest of their lives in the shadow of the traumatic experience. The longer the torment continues, the more likely their lives will be distorted by what has been done to them. For several years I was constantly aware that my movements, and my most intimate moments, were being monitored. As a result, I have developed an excessive interest in scrutinizing the secret lives of people. Though I have never observed people in a way that could be considered illegal, I have watched them very closely with the intention of unveiling what they might not have wished to reveal.

This must have been a factor in my decision to become a sociologist. At the time I wasn't aware that I was choosing a vocation that legitimated my obsession. As an undergraduate, I got sociology grades high enough to get me into graduate school and that, I thought, was why I chose the field. The fact that I was as familiar with Marx as my professors were should naturally have translated into an emphasis in Sociological Theory, but I was drawn to research that involved informal observation. Among other issues, I specialized in the use of unobtrusive research methods. While I never used cameras and rarely used recording devices, I engaged in long periods of covert surveillance of my subjects. Even as I write this I find myself falling into the terminology that we evolved to distance ourselves: why am I referring to *subjects* and not *people*?

When, as a graduate student, I wrote about or discussed the ethical issues involved in observing people I was, in an indirect way, trying to come to terms with what had been done to me. By what stretch of the imagination could the FBI agents who were following a pre-teen around New York have justified their behavior? Of course they were just doing a job, but someone had decided it was a job that needed to be done. Could anyone really have believed that following me somehow contributed to furthering national security? When I spied on a guy whose acquaintance I had made, and who trusted me, I justified the intrusion by telling myself that I would preserve his anonymity, that I was not damaging his world, and most importantly I was trying to learn something about human behavior. Did the FBI agents really believe that they weren't affecting my life? Was that how they justified what they did? Or were they merely harassing my mother and stepfather through me because they happened to be part of the Red Menace?

YOUTH

Downtown Community

PS 186 wasn't a great school, but by the time I wasn't the new kid anymore, I had figured out how to get by without calling attention to myself. That was no small achievement, and as the end of the school year approached, I began to worry about what was going to happen the following September. I was scheduled to move on to Stitt, the Junior High most 186 kids attended. Stitt had a reputation as a really tough school. Even though my friends from 186 would be there with me, they were going to have to prove how tough they were, and I was going to be an extra weight very few of them were going to want to carry. On top of that, Pete's trial was in the papers: fitting in was going to be next to impossible.

At the end of the year, when my report card revealed the fact that I had done no work, my mother decided it would be a good idea if I didn't go on to Stitt. She told me she would try to find a school that would be more sympathetic to a kid in my situation. I guessed she was thinking more in terms of politics than race but, no matter what she had in mind, the idea of not attending the local junior high appealed to my survival instincts. Anything was going to be better than Stitt.

When Rose made up her mind, there wasn't

much she wouldn't do to get her way. She met with the director of Downtown Community School, a private school on the Lower East Side. The director had left-wing sympathies, so her plea (I had no doubt tears were involved) convinced him to admit me on a full scholarship. In the fall, instead of attending the dreaded Stitt, I began taking the subway down to 11th Street and 2nd Avenue, where Downtown Community was located.

The director, Norman Studer, a former student of John Dewey, had established a curriculum at Downtown Community that relied heavily on experiential learning. It didn't take me long to discover that this philosophy fit my own agenda perfectly. It was exactly what I had been doing all along; it was just that at 186, the experience I was having was not one the teachers approved of.

Unlike me, most of my fellow students were already fairly well educated. Their parents had chosen the school for its unified curriculum that included a politics and arts emphasis. Some of my classmates came from elite environments: one was the son of the first black member of the President's cabinet; another was the son of a wealthy manufacturer; others were the children of professionals or artists. Most of us probably could have survived in normal classrooms, but not many of us would have flourished in those environments, certainly not as well as we did at Downtown Community.

Since the school's culture was thoroughly democratic, there wasn't one in-group that lauded it over the others. The curriculum reinforced egalitarianism: explicitly in the subjects we studied, but also in the way the school was organized. This made it easy for me to fit in, but it was also easy to avoid picking up the academic skills that most of the others had already acquired.

Even though I knew I lacked these skills, I was able to relax in this new environment. Once I left our apartment in the morning my weird life was behind me. On the subway downtown I would decompress, and by the time I got to school I was just another student. I missed my Harlem friends, and I was a little unsure of myself in this mostly white environment, but the curriculum was compelling, and the anti-school culture among the students—which had been so much a part of the daily life at PS 186—was so mild at Downtown Community that I never managed to get into serious trouble.

Pete had cut his political eyeteeth working on the Scottsboro case, so it wasn't an accident that one of the most strongly held views in our household was the idea that *black* not *white* women were far more likely to be sexually exploited. We believed that the prevailing stereotype that black men were sexual predators masked the fact that white men, particularly in the South, had almost unrestricted sexual access to black women. After hearing this a thousand times, just the thought of getting close to one of my female classmates at PS 186 produced so much guilt in me that I never had anything to do with any of them.

There was only one class per grade at DCS.

Since all of the girls in my class were white, on the first day of school I felt I had died and gone to heaven. From then on I began to do whatever I could to get female attention. Mostly I was obnoxious. My two teachers, Una Buxenbaum and Morris Salz, reacted to my behavior differently. She was warm, attractive, easy to like. He was a stern, remote disciplinarian. It was as if they had decided to create an ideal 1950's family constellation for kids like me. I don't think any of this was conscious; their personalities just happened to work that way. They were both smart people who, no doubt, had at least heard of Freud. My guess is they saw it for what it was, and figured it might work, and probably couldn't hurt with kids like me.

How wrong they were: I knew Salz was a lefty, and I was pretty sure he knew my history, so I knew his bark would be worse than his bite. At some point this all must have dawned on him, but by then it was too late: I was already at the top of his agenda and there was little, short of having me expelled, that he could do to bring me around. Actually, I had mixed feelings about him. Every once in a while I got the feeling he liked me. He always sucked on his pipe when he lectured me, even though the pipe was rarely lit, and he used that to control his temper, or at least to appear to be trying to do so. I knew he wanted to be seen as tough and compassionate. Aware that he was bluffing about the former trait, I took as much advantage of the latter as I could.

It seemed to me that all the adults who worked at Downtown Community were progressives. Pete

Seeger, who had been blacklisted for his politics, taught us music. The arts curriculum was linked with social studies. We took a field trip to visit farmers who were being evicted during the construction of the Downsville Dam, and when we returned we produced a play, with a mural depicting the displaced families as the set, and we sang songs based on our experience.

You might say we were learning history as it should be learned: as a deeply moving personal experience in which our own expressions had a role. But I was learning something even more important. I was beginning to think of myself as just another normal person, not as someone who had important things to hide. It wasn't as though all my private thoughts could now be easily expressed; I was too bottled up for that. But I didn't have to be constantly on guard; I was part of an essentially benevolent community, and knowing this helped me feel secure enough to begin to express some thoughts and feelings. My confusion about who I was hadn't disappeared: I knew I wasn't black, but I was pretty sure I wasn't white. This confusion remained with me throughout my time at Downtown Community but, at the very least, I was beginning to feel that I might be able to blend in with my people my age.

I made some friends and socialized with some of the guys after school. I got to see the inside of a Village townhouse. We went to parties at our classmates' apartments. I had a few crushes, some of which were mildly reciprocated, but none of these mostly imagined romances was anywhere near to being serious. Since the school was somewhat racially integrated, and that didn't appear to be a big deal for most students, I felt comfortable enough to reveal my family's racial profile to a few people. Given the Harlem accent that I had already acquired, I don't think my revelation was a great shock to anyone. Though the FBI was still putting pressure on my family by the time graduation approached I was beginning to feel almost normal.

Why do fools fall in love?

George Washington had almost lost the war in this part of Manhattan; so why they named the area and the high school after him was something I couldn't understand. I was excited about being in high school and a little worried. It was hard to find your way around a place this big. That was bad enough but when a giant guy blocked my progress in the hall I panicked.

"Is that you?" he asked. His face looked familiar, but I couldn't place him until he said, "It's me, man, Henry."

I couldn't believe it. This was not the skinny, bend-in-the-breeze Henry I had known in PS 186. This guy was almost six feet tall, and he had a chest that would make a tee shirt beg to be on him. He had been dragging one leg in a slow bop-walk, clearing a path in front of him that stretched way down the hall. The only thing about him that I recognized from the old Henry was that big smile. Only now, instead of making him look like some kind of pushover, his smile was like frost on an iceman.

Trying to match his cool, I made my body go loose. Even though I let go of every muscle, I knew I looked lame next to him. It was only because of old times that the two of us could even begin to have a conversation.

"No...that's not you, Henry. How did you get so tall, my man?"

"Hey, it happens. What are you up to?"

"Same old, same old." Then, because that sounded too sleepy, I added quickly, "You went on to Stitt, didn't you?"

He opened his eyes wide and nodded, I asked, "Was it as bad as they say?"

"Bad? That school was one total bad-ass situation from the get go."

He was talking loud enough for everyone in the hall to hear. He was proud of making it through Stitt. To have come out of there and still be able to tie your own shoelaces was saying something. I pulled out my pack of Pall Malls and held one out to him. He took it and motioned toward the bathroom.

When I pushed open the bathroom door our eyes met and we both knew the other had remembered. The bathroom was empty. I lit up, and as I let out a breath from the first puff, I told him my junior high experience hadn't been great, but I knew it was nothing like Stitt. I asked if he liked GW.

"It's different," he replied, a little smile starting to creep up his cheeks.

I knew he was referring to the fact that white people went here. "I noticed that," I said. "The air is lighter this far uptown. It's like being in the country."

He laughed and said, "You've never been in the country."

By sounding on me like that he was letting me know we were still tight. A group of guys came through the door. One of them, even taller than

Henry, looked at us and made it clear he couldn't figure out what we were doing.

Henry said to him, "He's cool, man; I know him from 186."

Henry nodded at the guy and then at me. "Sherman, this is Richie."

Sherman held out his hand with his palm up and I tapped it with my knuckles. Sherman seemed to think the greeting was smooth enough, and he went over to the group that had formed in the corner. They gathered in a circle and they all bent their heads together until their foreheads were almost touching. They just stood there bent over in this little circle, not saying a word, looking like they were searching for something on the floor. Then Sherman started singing in this deep bass voice.

Hey, tumba, tumba, tumba, toe.

I felt each note before I actually heard it. These were the deepest sounds I had ever heard coming out of a human being. The sound didn't start in his throat; it was drawn from deep down inside him, like it had been rolling around in his stomach for a while before it was ready to come out into the open air.

Everyone laughed. Then Sherman said, "Let's hit it again."

As they were leaning over to put their heads together again, Henry whispered, "He made a record, but it hasn't been released yet."

Sherman started in again, and he hit the same exact notes he had sung before. This time they all must have thought it was fine because, when he reached *toe* there was a pause, and then everyone came in with: *oo-wa, oo-wa, oo oo-wa-aa, oo-wa.*

Their voices reminded me of the operas Uncle Pat would listen to on the radio on Sundays. You couldn't understand the words; all you could hear was the music in the singer's voice. This was like that; each voice had a little different pitch, and as they went up and down the notes, you could feel the harmony. My chest was tingling from all the sound bouncing off the tile in that bathroom. It was the perfectness of the interval between the voices that made me tingle, like when a crystal glass cracks because the sound waves are lined up just right.

Then Sherman sang: *Why do fo—ols fall in lo—ve?*

The last part of *love* was so sweet, I felt like I might never come across anything this perfect again in my whole life. Then the singing stopped and everyone was talking all at once, saying how good it sounded and how they should do more. They gathered together again in the corner. Sherman took his time, like he was waiting for some spirit that needed to come into him before he could start. Part of me could almost feel the spirit; another part of me was saying, *Come on, Sherman it's not all that great.*

It was a performance, as if they were onstage at the Apollo performing to a full house. Finally Sherman started up again, and they went into the harmony. They were holding the notes a little longer this time, adjusting their voices. One guy had his hand out like he was about to dribble a basketball. He raised his hand a couple of inches, and they went up to the next note. He held them there a while and then he started dragging his hand slowly to the side, making them slide into the next note. Once they were there, he tensed his hand to get them to hold it.

The door opened and a man who was as tall as Sherman stood there in the doorway. Henry whispered, "That's Tillson, the principal."

I was the only one smoking. I chucked what was left of my cigarette into the toilet and flushed it. My heart was pounding. I knew the principal couldn't miss the cloud of smoke around me. I had just been in on a great scene with a down bunch of amazing guys, and now I was going to get my ass kicked in front of them. I made up my mind that I wouldn't lose face, even if it meant getting suspended.

The principal looked in my direction, but his eyes went right past me without stopping. He backed up and held the door open without saying a word and everyone piled out into the hall. As I passed him, he gave me a look that let me know I was marked. Probably the surprise of seeing a white guy in there had kept him from doing anything. I knew I wouldn't be this lucky the next time around.

The curriculum at Downtown Community hadn't been organized along departmental lines so the program of classes I was assigned at George Washington bore no relation to the academic skills I had acquired. That was merely the icing on an already tottering cake. The truth was that GW, like practically every other high school in America, had two tracks. Even if my skill set had matched the college bound track perfectly, which it by no stretch of the imagination did, I was far too interested in the non-academic culture of the school to have been a scholastic success. It wasn't long before I was cutting class regularly.

Grandma's funeral

We were outside the funeral home. I had just lied to my mother; I told her that I wanted to wait outside in the car because I didn't want to look at Grandma's body.

My mother wasn't buying it. "Grandma doesn't exist anymore. The body in there isn't Grandma. Try to remember what she was like when she was alive. That will help you get through it."

When she was alive all she did was complain. If by some miracle she had come back to life, and was in the car with us now, she wouldn't say hello; she would start right in complaining about how much the funeral cost, and how many people hadn't shown up, and then she would go into a song and dance about how much pain she was in. My mother was acting like she had never seen Grandma in operation.

Then Rose tried another way of getting to me. "You look so handsome in your new suit. Don't you want people to see it?"

She knew me. I did look great in my new suit. My mother gave me the money, and I bought it down on 42nd near 8th. The jacket had an ivy-league three button cut and the material was black wool with these little gray hairs blending in. Charcoal gray, it was called. It was low key with the white shirt I was wearing now; the guy in the store had shown me how it looked with a pink shirt and that had done it. He was the same guy who had sold me my electric blue pegged pants with double saddle side stitching.

As much as I wanted to show off the suit I didn't want to be seen by the people in the funeral home. It had nothing to do with me being afraid of Grandma's body. It was Pete's coming in there with us that made me want to be somewhere—anywhere—else. He was out on bail. When he went in there everyone was going to take his showing up as an insult to Grandma. That was why my mother had suddenly forgotten Grandma's bad points: she was about to wreck Grandma's funeral.

I figured they would try to keep him out, and he would try to push his way in, and one thing would lead to another. When someone did a knuckle drill on him, Pete would fight back and my mother would do something crazy just to up the ante. It was a nightmare waiting to happen, and I didn't even have the beginning of a plan of what I would do.

"They don't want us in there. Can't we just skip it?" I knew my mother wouldn't be happy with my saying that, but it was my last shot.

"She's my mother and I have a right to be there, and my husband has a right to be with me."

"Grandma isn't going to be there. You said that yourself. The funeral is for them; why not let them have it?"

"They're bigots, and I'm not going to let them run my life."

The thing was my mother was stubborn. What

had set her off was that Aunt Mary had made all the arrangements without asking for her advice. I guess since Aunt Mary took care of Grandma, she felt she had the right to decide how Grandma should be remembered. It was pretty obvious she was also getting back at my mother for not helping to take care of Grandma.

The door of the funeral home opened, and Grandpa came out. I had never seen him in a suit and tie. His chest and stomach seemed too large for any suit, not to mention the one he had on. All I could see was a big spread of white that poked out between the lapels of his suit-coat. He came straight across the street over to where our driver had parked the car. He opened Big Pete's door and held out his hand and they shook. I could tell they had never met before.

Grandpa said, "You come inside with me." Then he added, "Rosa, you take Richie."

As much as I wanted to be someplace else, there was no getting out of it now. Before he came over, I figured that if I didn't budge they might leave me in the car with the driver. Now, with Grandpa helping Pete, even if I didn't budge my mother could drag me. The idea of people watching her pull me along was enough to get me going. We all did what Grandpa had said. As far as I knew, it was the first time that anyone had ever listened to him.

In a way he had a right to be in charge of the funeral. Aunt Mary had been closer to Grandma. Grandpa and Grandma Manosia didn't even sleep in the same room, but they had known one another almost as long as Grandma had been alive. They had come across an ocean and raised children together. Grandpa's life was almost over. Even if Aunt Mary never got married she would still have a good part of her life left to get to know other people. This was it for him.

There were a few men standing near the door to the funeral parlor. I didn't recognize any of them. As we got nearer, I could see they were wearing American Legion hats. I couldn't understand why they were here. The Manosias never had anything to do with the American Legion. When we got close to them, Pete's shoulders went back and he moved out in front of Grandpa. I could tell my mother was scared because she started squeezing my hand. I tried to pull away, but she tightened her grip. There was no way I wanted one arm tied up, so I told her she was hurting my hand and she let go. She probably realized that we were both better off with our hands free.

Pete was only a few yards from the door. The men had all come together in a knot to block the entrance. Pete turned a little to one side and lowered his shoulder like a battering ram. I could tell his plan wasn't going to work; a couple of these guys were pretty big. I wanted to run, but as scared as I was, I couldn't see leaving them there without at least trying to help. My mother grabbed my shoulders to keep me from going forward. Now, at least, there was a chance they might treat my mother and me like spectators. It was cowardly to feel good about that, but I couldn't help feeling it. I just wanted us to be safe. My relief didn't last: I quickly realized that once they started beating on Pete, Rose would get involved.

Then Grandpa shouted, "Aspetta."

Pete stopped in his tracks. The men in the doorway looked surprised. I couldn't tell if it was because Pete had understood Grandpa or just that Grandpa had taken charge. While the Legionnaires were figuring out what to do, Grandpa went around in front of Pete and started toward the door. Pete followed behind him, and my mother and I brought up the rear. When Grandpa reached the men they parted, and because Grandpa was so wide Pete slipped in behind him. My mother pushed my shoulders, and we all marched single file through the door, and the lobby, into the main room.

There were about twenty people sitting in folding chairs. I recognized some of our neighbors, but none of my father's family was there. Aunt Mary was sitting in the front row. She had turned around, and she was staring at my mother like she hated the ground my mother walked on. I could feel everyone's eyes on us. I understood that most of them probably felt sorry for me but that didn't help. I knew some of them probably thought we were garbage. If my mother knew what they were thinking, she didn't let on. In order to want to come here, she couldn't even begin to worry about what they were thinking. She hated them as much as they hated her. When I thought about the men who had blocked the doorway I could see where her hatred was coming from. But not everyone was like those men.

There were some empty seats in the front row, and Grandpa led us all the way there and sat down.

Pete sat next to him, and I sat between him and my mother. Being next to Pete meant I would be right in the line of fire if someone took a shot at him. The hair on the back of my neck must have been standing up straight. I felt like, any minute, a bullet was going to slam into the back of my head. There would be plenty of guys in Bensonhurst who would be happy to pull the trigger on Pete.

We sat there with nothing happening. It was just total silence. Grandma's casket was just in front of us. She was lying there with her arms crossed over her chest. The light on her was at an angle, and it made her wrinkles look like a lace curtain draped on the skin of her hands and face. You could feel the energy in the room, but Grandma, in the middle of all that, was just as peaceful as she could be. In her whole life she had never spent a moment looking as calm as this.

Then Grandpa got up and started talking in Italian. I had trouble understanding what he was saying because he was crying. It had something to do with coming over from Italy. Finally he just stopped and started sobbing. No one knew what to do, so we all waited. He apologized and sat down. Aunt Mary got up and said Grandma had been brave for suffering through so much pain. She said she would miss Grandma. How she could miss someone who had made her life so miserable was beyond me. It wasn't just the constant moaning or the *get me this and get me that* she had to put up with; it was the fact that Grandma wouldn't let Aunt Mary have a life of her own. How could you miss that? But for some reason I believed her. Maybe it was because she was afraid of being on her own, and Grandma had given her an excuse for staying home all the time.

Then Aunt Mary told everyone there was food at the back of the room, and she thanked the people who had brought it. I knew this was a way of getting at my mother because she hadn't brought anything and everyone knew it. When she sat down I figured it was pretty much over. I could hear chairs scraping behind me: people were getting up. My mother got up and stood next to the casket facing the crowd. She started talking but people weren't listening so she started shouting.

"My sister is right. My mother was a brave woman. She was brave because she was willing to leave the life she had known in Italy in order to come to America, a place where even the most simple things, like shopping or using the telephone, were strange and difficult. In the rush to fit in, to become good Americans, the great risks that our ancestors took should not be forgotten. We are not descended from a nation of racists and bigots."

Someone in the back shouted, "Sit down and shut up."

My mother didn't bat an eye. "Are you afraid of what I have to say?"

Another voice said, "Don't you have no respect for the dead?"

By this time almost everyone was standing. Most people were heading for the food and making it clear they weren't going to listen to my mother. My mother would have gone on shouting except that she looked over at Pete, and he shook his head and gave her a look that said, "Don't bother." She shut up and came over to us. Pete got up and so did I. My mother got behind me and started pushing my shoulders toward the door. She didn't have to bother; I was as ready for some fresh air as I would ever be. When we got outside, one of the Legionnaires shoved Pete, and Pete shoved back. The guy was about to take a swing when one of his friends caught his arm and held him back.

The driver had been told to stay with the car, and he did his duty, holding the door open for us when we got there. We all got in: Pete in front, and my mother and me in back. As we drove away, I felt as though my life had just been given back to me. Maybe it had been spared; Pete's, sure as hell, had been.

The Apollo

You had to climb a flight of stairs to get to the poolroom. When we reached the top we saw the place was almost empty. Henry pointed to a table in the corner that he said was level. I should have known better than to gamble with him; he was way ahead of my game but we were just playing for time, and that was the rock bottom price you could pay for the education I was about to receive. And there was always the chance I might get lucky (in my heart I knew that was about as likely as winning the Irish sweepstakes without a ticket).

We lagged for break and I won. I aimed high on the cue ball. I knew, from the way my stick felt when it connected with the ball—smooth and soft, like the way a bow would bend for an arrow, only much faster—that I had connected right. My whole body was moving behind the stroke and the energy just kept going through my arm into the stick, and the cue ball, and on into the pack, and through the first ball into each one as the pack burst apart across the table. Two balls disappeared in the pockets at the other end.

I tried not to let my excitement show as the balls rolled down the gutters. I checked the table: I couldn't tell right off if I had a better chance with high or low. My whole game had to be position; if I left him a shot he would probably run the table. I figured if I missed the three ball, I might still leave him safe. Sure enough when I tried to bank the three it went dead in the cushion, but I hadn't left him a shot.

Henry was chewing his gum loudly as he chalked up. As he bent for his shot I could almost feel him thinking ahead to the eight ball. It looked like there was no finesse in his game; everything was straight ahead. That was the come on; in fact, his first shot opened up the whole table. As he ran out the high balls he was still chewing like mad, only now he was smiling. Somehow every shot was easy. He didn't give me another shot until I had racked twice. He was showing me his real stuff. It was a privilege other guys would have had to pay big bucks to witness.

When he was done, he helped me put the balls in the tray and he walked with me over to the counter. The guy stamped the card and I paid. As we headed downstairs, Henry asked if I wanted to smoke some reefer. I was ashamed to tell him I had never done it. I wasn't even sure of what you were supposed to do. It was already long past the time I should have been getting home if I hadn't cut school. I told him that.

He said, "Too bad. I was going to do a joint and head over to the Apollo."

Though I had been hearing about the Apollo since PS 186 and I was dying to go there, I had blown all my money paying for our time. When I told Henry I couldn't afford the Apollo he said that he had just hit the number and he would lend me the money. I was pretty sure the number hadn't come out yet, but I didn't see any point in challenging him and I told him

I could pay him back next week. We both knew that was a lie.

He lit up the joint, took a drag and passed it to me. I followed suit. As we walked toward the subway I did my best to notice changes in how I was feeling. The only difference was that I felt really light on my feet. Each step I took seemed to happen without my legs having anything to do with it. We went down into the subway. To get to the downtown train we had to walk through a tunnel. I noticed, as we walked along, that the tiles on the wall seemed to be zipping by but we weren't getting any closer to the end of the tunnel.

I was scared; time and space weren't working the way they usually did: they both seemed to be going in the same direction. Henry was walking backwards in front of me. He had a hand on each of my shoulders; he was looking me in the eye and he was saying, "You got to get a hold of yourself son."

He smiled and a huge wave of relief broke over me. We both started laughing. I looked down at the end of the tunnel again. The end hadn't come any closer, but now it didn't matter. We could stay there walking in the tunnel forever.

I heard the train pulling into the station. Henry started running and I followed. We were flying along. All of a sudden Henry let out a scream, and the people getting off the train parted. He got to the door just as it was closing; he put an arm in and when the conductor opened the door again we both piled in. We stood in the middle of the car acting goofy and cracking up. Nobody seemed to mind. It was like the whole crowd in the car had picked up on our good mood.

When we got to 125th Street Henry rubbed his hands together and shouted, *"Show Time."* We went downstairs from the El and started walking east. We passed a bottle club on the corner. One of the guys had a paper bag held up to his mouth. I said, "What's the word?" and he chimed right back with "Thunderbird." When he looked over at me he didn't seem surprised to see me, and he held out the bag. I wanted to take a taste but Henry was moving fast so I thanked the guy and kept going.

"That sneaky Pete will rot your brain, my man."

He was talking to me like I was a kid and I almost told him to cool the preaching; after all, he was the one who was holding the dope. Instead I kept my mouth shut and we just cruised 125th like two glider planes next to one another letting the wind set their course. It wasn't long before I could see the Apollo marquee up ahead. People were standing in line to buy tickets. I had heard that white people came uptown to see the shows but they wouldn't be my age, dressed like me, or buying balcony tickets. I was pleased that no one seemed to notice me.

Henry paid and we went upstairs to the way back. The show had already started. An old fat lady was on stage singing.

Once I lived the life of a millionaire/

She was doing a grind that was supposed to be sexy, and in a certain way it was. She was wearing a tight red dress that had no sleeves or shoulder straps. She was just about exploding out of it. When she leaned down toward the people in the front row and shook her shoulders everyone went wild. Even the women were shouting; everyone was laughing and acting like they were really turned on by her. Pretty soon everyone in our section was on their feet and moving.

...spending my money; I didn't care/

People were shouting and singing with her. Most of the voices were up over hers but one or two men managed to get lower. It was like watching a fountain with water that bubbled up higher or lower when you least expected it. As soon as one person would finish you could feel how his or her part fit in with the whole. It was the slow bass and drum rhythm that was cueing it. Each beat had many tiny accents that a person could follow. There was a quick beat after *money*: one of those pauses that had to remain empty. Everyone understood that; I could feel the quick breath being taken and then the rush of sound that followed.

...taking my friends out for a mighty fine time/

The drummer just slammed down hard once and then everything stopped. Then she started talking to the audience, like she was having a conversation with one person.

...You know what a good time is don't you honey?

She did a little shimmy, then a grind, and then a couple of bumps. She was just doing it, acting like there was some guy right there on stage with her. She made us all feel, men and women alike, that she could take us all on. There was that much energy in her. People started shouting, "*Yes, mamma*" and "*Do it, honey.*" There couldn't be a person in the whole place who didn't feel it.

I looked over at Henry; his eyes were swollen but there were no tears. The whole room was full of joy—only the joy was tinged with sadness. It had something to do with the fact that a person you might have thought was ugly had transformed herself into the opposite. While you understood that you also knew when the lights came up the ugliness would still be there.

...drinking high priced liquor, Champagne, and wine.

I started singing along with her. The next thing I knew the lights had gone out, and we were all sitting there in the dark. My throat was sore and my hands hurt. I had been screaming and clapping for some time. As we waited for the next act I thought about the performance I had just been a part of. Was it the dope or had it been as moving as I had thought?

An over-amplified voice blasted out, *I put a spell on you.*

A spotlight came up on the center of the stage; a tall man was standing there. He was dressed entirely in white: shoes, socks, pants, vest, shirt, tie, and tails. Dangling from his shoulders, and draped out behind him on the floor, was the longest white cape I had ever seen. He ran toward the edge of the stage and then he jumped off into the blackness with the cape flying behind him. The spotlight caught up with him and followed him up the aisle. I watched until he disappeared under the balcony. He reappeared a minute later down another aisle running toward the stage.

When he first appeared I had been stunned by the way he looked. Then, when he was running around, the band kept vamping; they were playing the same chord build up over and over. The same thump, thump, thump, of the rhythm became boring. I turned to Henry and he must have felt the same way because he said, "All show and no music."

That was exactly right. The audience seemed to be eating it up though; they were acting pretty much the same way they had when the fat lady was on. Couldn't they tell the difference? The guy was sweating up a storm, but his routine was basically a clown act.

Someone hollered, "Where did you get that cape?"

"His mamma's looking for some new curtains."

A woman near us shouted, "Hell, his mamma's a nurse. She can't go to work cause he stole her stockings."

"If he keeps running around like that his *do* will fall off."

"That ain't no *do* that's conk crete."

"That boy left his head in the oven too long,

done burnt the cee-ment."

"Give the man a break."

"Don't need no break, the man needs an act."

By now I was sure he could hear the yelling in the balcony and I was beginning to feel sorry for him. People began shouting all over the theater. The band cranked up the volume but the crowd just got louder. It was like being in a riot; everyone was yelling, or cracking up, and totally out of control. We were having a ball.

Then over all the other voices a woman shouted, "Melvin, take off that stupid wig and come home this minute."

That was it. We all lost it. Melvin, or whoever he was, just shrugged and walked off-stage. There were tears in my eyes from so much laughing. After a while, Henry got enough control of himself to say we should split. I was feeling so at home that I wanted to hang around to enjoy the scene longer but Henry had paid my way and I couldn't let him leave without me. I told him that next time I would cover the tickets. We both knew that wasn't going to happen.

A Marxist Contradiction

Pete, along with most of the top Communist Party leadership, had been indicted under the Smith Act. This law, passed in 1940, made it a crime to teach or advocate the violent overthrow of the U.S. government. Though sections of the law were later found to be in violation of the first amendment, the Smith Act was never repealed.

The indictment of these leaders presented the Communist Party with a difficult choice. Communists had always argued that the government supported the interests of the upper class. They were quick to point out that U.S. history was replete with examples of egalitarian movements that had been met with violence, and that the violence was either sanctioned or perpetrated by the government. Most of the leaders had publicly stated that violence would be inevitable if socialism were ever to come to America.

Pete, and the other indicted Party leaders, had a choice: they could argue that they hadn't meant what they said, or they could defend their right to say it. Arguing for one's free speech rights didn't directly contradict the idea that the government operated in the interests of capitalism, but it certainly undercut that kind of revolutionary rhetoric. And taking the other tack, that violence hadn't been advocated, would have been perceived as hypocritical. There was no obvious way out of this dilemma so the indicted leaders tried to finesse the issue by attacking the system. Pete, acting as his own lawyer, took responsibility for making the case against a social system that exploited Negroes. In his opening statement to the jury he said:

We intend to show that far from advocating force and violence, our Party has fought for the constitutional right to vote for the millions of Negro men and women who still remain disfranchised in the poll tax states of the South; that it has fought against exclusion of Negroes from governmental and political posts on all levels, and for their constitutional right to hold all elective and appointive political posts.

We intend to show that this program of guaranteeing the right of the Negro people to vote in the poll tax states in the South, serves the democratic interests of the entire nation in that it will, among other things, insure the removal of the antidemocratic representatives in Congress who dominate key positions in the House and Senate.

We intend to show that our consistent fight for Negro representation on all levels is not a conspiratorial act, is not based on force and violence, but is aimed to realize in life the 13th, 14th, and 15th Amendments to our Constitution – to realize full and equal citizenship for the Negro people.

This ladies and gentlemen of the jury, has been my main responsibility as secretary of the National Negro Commission [of the Communist Party]. Jointly with Benjamin J. Davis, its chairman, it was my responsibility to bring these relevant facts to broad sections of the white people and to help to the best of my ability to encourage and inspire the Negro people to have confidence in the white workers, middle class and poor farmers; confidence in the ability of these people to understand this question and to participate with and assist the Negro people in breaking through these political, economic and social barriers.

We intend to show that this fight for Negro representation, the fight against Jim Crow in all of its forms throughout the country, the fight against lynching, the fight against the poll tax, the fight for equal opportunities for Negro men and women, is part of the fight for self-determination of the Negro people in the Black Belt.

The war against fascism was over, and the Soviet Union was no longer an ally. The prosecutions under the Smith Act took place while U.S. soldiers were fighting a war against Communists in Korea. Given the political situation and the wording of the Smith Act, it wasn't surprising that the juries in all of these trials found the defendants guilty. Pete was given a three-year sentence which he began serving at the Federal Correctional Facility in Danbury Connecticut.

In my experience, none of the Communists I had met was prone to violence. I never heard any of them discuss, much less actually plan to perpetrate, a violent act. Violence as a means of self-defense, however, was definitely a position that Pete, and probably most of his comrades, advocated. Unfortunately, in prison, not all of the leaders were able to defend themselves. Robert Thompson, who had earned the Distinguished Service Cross for bravery during World War two, was attacked in prison and nearly murdered.

Birdland

Jumpin with my boy Sid in the city, president of the DJ committee, got to be Prez, Bird, Shearing, or the Basie...

One of those crazy people who hang out around Times Square had been singing Sid's song. From there, all the way up to Birdland, I couldn't get it out of my head. I had been listening to Sid for months on my Emerson portable radio. The portable was about the size of a tissue box, maybe half as tall, encased in yellowing plastic. At night, I would curl up under the covers with it next to my ear and listen until I fell asleep. It would warm that side of my face, and the sounds that it sent my way were something else.

Sid was another terrific music teacher. It wasn't any kind of formal education. He just played the most wonderful music ever recorded. Listening to it, I learned to tell the great from the good. It was the best kind of education: there weren't going to be any tests so I didn't need to know the names. Though, over time, you couldn't help knowing who was playing what. It was pretty clear the whole point was just to be in the moment. I hadn't thought any of this through; it was just what it was.

What I did know was that Sid, the ultimate hipster, had found a way of turning night into day. I identified with him because he was a white man airing black people's music. Not just any music: not popular music, not rock and roll, not blues; he only played the refined, urbane form of black music, definitely not easy listening. On the edges, it could be so complex you couldn't hear it until you had been exposed to it many times around.

It was listening to Sid's show that had started me coming to Birdland. You just knew the music had to be listened to live. The club was in the basement. Every time I had come down those stairs a very short fat guy had been waiting at the bottom to show me a table. He dressed like a man, but there was something about him that gave me the feeling he might be a woman. Probably it was the high pitched voice, or just that I wanted it to be that way, mysterious, like Cerberus guarding the way into Hades. It was pretty clear he could only exist down there; sunlight probably would have killed him. But it wasn't hell I was descending toward; it was the exact opposite.

He never let on that he knew I was underage and he remembered, probably because I always tipped him, that I liked to sit as far back from the music as I could get. It wasn't because of my age that I sat away from the center of the action. Compared to most of the people in this room, I was pretty much of a square and I didn't want to be showing my squareness off. These night people, as Gene Shepard (another radio hipster) called them, were of different types. There were black men and women, maybe they worked at the PO or had some other steady job, and were out for the evening. There were tourists: out-of-towners and foreigners who might have fallen into the place by mistake or who had come there because they had fallen for the music. Then there were the hipsters, black and white: mostly broke and living on the edge. They were friendly, but you had to be careful with them: they could scheme on you in ways that wouldn't quit. While you were down here, the rules of the world upstairs went by the wayside. That was just fine with me.

The band had just finished a number, and everyone was still clapping as I sat down. A voice—I couldn't tell which of the musicians was talking—said, "We're going to close this set with Doodlin." A few people clapped and the piano player nodded.

Then the pianist started playing all by himself. He sprinkled a few notes at us and then he stopped dead. The pause begged for an answer and, sure enough, the rest of the band, trumpet, sax, bass, and drums, all hit the same note perfectly and kept moving until they had finished their response. Then the piano hit the first part again, and the band did the whole thing over. Then he moved it up a notch, it seemed like he had changed octaves, and the others answered in the new octave, or wherever they were, again.

At first the music felt very loose, like the notes were falling by chance. Then the drummer started keeping a very steady march and the horns were all parading around inside the original pattern that the piano had laid down. Even though it sounded loose it was about as far from accident as you could get.

Someone yelled. "Hit it Spider." All along, the piano player had been hunched over the keyboard, with his head bent low and his elbows up. The nickname described him perfectly.

A school named for the slave owning Jefferson

"The Jefferson School is a school for all working people, Negro and white. It is dedicated to meeting their needs and advancing their interests. It is open to everyone, regardless of color or nationality, creed or political belief no matter how much or how little their previous schooling.

"The Jefferson School is a Marxist school. It teaches Marxism as the philosophy and social science of the working class. It emphasizes the distinctive features of the development of the United States, its democratic traditions, its cultural heritage, and the militant history of the American working class and the Negro people.

"It is the aim of the Jefferson School to encourage students to think for themselves and to reach their own reasoned conclusions. ...

"The first step after you have resolved to master Marxism is to be convinced that you can do so. The capitalist class does not want you to gain this self-confidence."

Whenever I thought about people who were really poor, an intense feeling of sadness would come over me, and then I would usually tell myself I had to do something. The problem was that I had been around enough poor people to know that helping an individual who is destitute is like bailing a sinking ship with a teacup: it might make you feel you were accomplishing something, but it wasn't going to change the overall situation. It was pretty clear that if I was going to make a difference I needed to know more about how economics and politics worked.

My mother had been pressuring me to take a course at the Jefferson School. My feelings about doing so were mixed: while I felt guilty about not doing anything when there was so much suffering— and I wanted to understand how this repulsive situation had come about—I also wanted to enjoy my life. Going downtown, at night, to take a class was not my idea of fun.

Nevertheless, after dragging my feet, I finally signed up for a class. The other students weren't like me: a grimmer bunch of people would have been hard to find, and the program itself was as far from a barrel of laughs as you could get. Still, reading that line: "*to master Marxism is to be convinced that you can do so,*" really struck a cord. At Downtown Community I had acquired, for the first time (outside of sports), a sense that I could actually do something really difficult, and do it well. I knew that science was difficult, and a science of society had to be as hard as any subject ever gets, yet, somehow, I felt I was up to the task.

It didn't take me long to grasp the labor theory of value. The fight over wages had to be a big deal in the way an economy functioned. That it provided the engine that motivated much of modern history was a real eye opener. I saw how it was related to other aspects of Marxism: materialism, the role of the state, the stages of history, false consciousness; even what was called the national question (the race issue) was of a piece with the rest of the theory. It all fit together: philosophy, economics, history; even art could be understood through Marxism. I was beginning to see that it was an approach that could make sense of any situation.

I was one of the youngest students at the Jefferson School and I had never seriously studied an academic subject. Thanks to the twins, and the other risks in the neighborhood, I had spent more time reading than most kids my age but almost everything I had read was fiction. Even though I was unprepared academically, perhaps *because* I was unprepared, I grasped the material easily. I found that reading economic and philosophic tracts, and making sense of them, wasn't a big deal.

I enjoyed the lively discussions with my fellow classmates. I fancied myself quite the dialectical logician. I didn't really mind that my schoolmates changed my name. In class, and then later in most political and social circles, I was no longer Richie Rizzo; I had become Richie Perry. I liked my new name. It had cache' among the Party people, and it obscured my ethnicity. *Perry* could be anything; it wasn't a provincial name, the way Rizzo was.

The name change was linked with a change in how I saw myself. At the Jefferson School I was an insider. Formerly I had thought of myself as an isolate; now I felt that I was a part of something, not a well-defined group, but I was aware of a pool of people all over the world who understood life in a certain way, and who would, almost instinctively, support one another. I felt I was in the secret center of that world; I understood the language; I knew the operational principles; I had the pedigree; and most of all, I had clear insight into what mattered.

It would seem to be a contradiction to suggest that while I felt all this about my new identity, I also felt, as I grew into this new self, a distance from the persona that I was constructing. I was getting an education, and I was beginning to see myself as an educated person, at least in this particular tradition, but I believed in Marxism—and didn't believe in it— at the same time. This is much the way a child *feels* about the world of caretakers: the parental world is embraced and viewed from afar at the same time. Eventually the child separates from this family of orientation and becomes a mature adult or in rare tragic situations the child's development ceases.

Jail

When I told my mother that I didn't want to visit Pete she started crying. Then, when she realized that approach wasn't going to work, she went into this song and dance about how they were trying to break his spirit, and I was helping them. She was cultivating a garden she had toiled in many times before, but this time she had some truth on her side; my guilt kicked in, and I told her I would go.

The jail was in Danbury, Connecticut. Even before the train had pulled out of the station I could feel my neck getting stiff. By the time we were at the front gate, I could barely hold my head up. A guard gave my mother a piece of paper and told us to follow him. Then we went inside. When I heard the door lock behind us everything around me started swirling. My legs were carrying me deeper into the jail but my insides were screaming to be let out.

To keep from fainting I focused on a big sign on the wall. The sign said that it was a felony to bring firearms and narcotics into the prison. My mother's harping on how they would do anything to break Pete had me primed for something exactly like this. What if they planted something on us? I tried to tell myself that I was being paranoid, but the truth was I had no way of knowing what they might do.

As we started down a long corridor I could see a set of bars at the other end. When we got a few feet from them there was a loud crashing noise and they slid apart. A guard on the other side controlled the gate, and I could tell that he enjoyed watching the fear that this sudden noise had set off in us. We went through that gate and the first guard said, "Perry 12705," or something like that. He stayed behind while the gate closed on us. Another gate opened on the other side. I felt like we were in a submarine and had just gone through the air lock. The air-lock guard told us to take the door on the right.

So far, except for the bars at the end of each corridor, the place looked like the inside of a hospital. The hallway we were walking down was spotless; there was no chipped paint and the floors were as shiny as a pair of patent leather shoes. What made it different from a hospital was that there were no pictures on the walls and there was no furniture. It was just a plain corridor with fluorescent lights on the ceiling—not old, not dirty—just empty and boring.

The door on our right opened into a room that looked like a school cafeteria, except that the windows were up high near the ceiling. Formica tables were set up around the room and people were sitting at the tables talking. In one corner, up on a high platform, there was a guard seated at a desk. From there he could see everything that went on in the room.

The guards all wore hats that made them look like bus drivers. I had been half expecting the prisoners to be wearing stripes but they were wearing blue denim work shirts and dungarees. I was glad that Pete wouldn't be dressed up in a monkey suit.

Most of the prisoners in the room were white. Up to this time, I had expected that there would be a lot of Negro prisoners, and that they would protect Pete. Now I wasn't as sure about that. There didn't seem to be enough of them in this prison. I had heard that Danbury was known as the Country Club because only the less dangerous criminals were housed here.

It would have been hard for me to visit a white person in jail, but I could have done it. I even could have visited Pete if all the prisoners were Negroes. But being a mixed family in this scene was impossible. In this weird place, with all these weird people, I was the weirdest thing of all, a freak among freaks. The fact that escape from the place was impossible heightened my sense that I was highly visible. There was no way I could disappear in here.

We went up to the guard, and my mother handed him the paper the first guard had given her. He yelled as loudly as he could. "Perry … 12705."

I never would have suspected that someone shouting at the top of his lungs like that could sound so completely cold. Something told me he knew who Perry was. Probably the word had gone around among the guards as soon as we showed up at the front gate. I knew one thing: all the time that we would be sitting there this cracker wouldn't be able to think about anything except my mother and Pete in bed together. You couldn't miss the hatred in his gaze as he watched us from his pedestal.

If I had it in my power to erase people, he would have been gone from the earth without a trace, but the truth was I didn't have the power to do shit.

In his eyes, I was something you couldn't quite ignore, something you hoped would go away, yet something you wouldn't bother to lift a finger to erase. When he looked at me I could tell he wanted to flush me down a toilet. I closed my eyes to release myself from the grip of his stare.

I must have been standing there for at least two minutes with my eyes shut. I opened them when I felt my mother's hand tugging at my arm. Pete had come into the room. As the three of us walked over to one of the tables, I noticed that the conversations around us had stopped. Before we sat down my mother threw her arms around Pete and gave him a hug and kiss. She couldn't have known if the rules allowed you to touch; it was just like her to push it. Nobody said anything. Then the guard cleared his throat, and Pete took her by the shoulders and sat her down opposite him. I went over and sat next to her.

As the conversations in the room resumed, Pete and mom sat there talking like they were out for a picnic. I couldn't follow what they were saying. All I could think about were all the strangers, convicted criminals every one of them, maybe even murderers, watching us. I could just about feel what they were thinking. These guys weren't in here for helping old ladies to cross the street, and we were just the kind of event that could set one of them off. Later, when they went back to their cells, the entire prison would know the story. It would spread from this room, like the threads of a giant spider web, until it covered the whole place. Only there would be two webs: one black and the other white.

I couldn't tell whether anyone was going to make any moves. There were about twenty-five people in the room; in addition to Pete there was only this one other Negro inmate who was being visited by his wife and baby. He was a strong looking guy, but I didn't think he would be any help; the baby tied his hands. I heard Pete's voice saying my name and it sounded like it had come at the end of a question. I looked over at him, indicating that I didn't understand, and he repeated. "I said, are you enjoying high school, Richie?"

I realized that my mother had written him about me, and I felt guilty about not writing, so I apologized for that. Pete acted like he didn't mind, and he asked me again. Since the truth was I hadn't been attending school much, I was having trouble thinking about what to say. All I could get out was. "It's not bad."

Pete looked me in the eye and started talking "I'm working in the laundry. The younger men do the really hard work. I just give out clothing, Manny, over there," he nodded toward a white guy in the corner, "is in charge of our operation. He used to keep the books for a big corporation. His boss was cheating the tax collector, and Manny ended up in here."

He was letting us know he had become part of the life in here and that there were white people in here who were civilized enough to be friendly toward him. I was relaxed enough to say. "I bet he's pissed off."

Pete shrugged as he spoke. "Not really. He'll be getting out soon. Some of the guys say he'll be able to retire for life when he gets out."

I could see where Pete was headed. He had some moral in mind about Manny being an exploited wage slave and jail just being part of the whole corrupt system. I was about to jump on his theory when I realized it was just his way of making conversation. This was no time to pick a fight with him. I started to tell him about a part-time job I was thinking of getting when my mother jumped in with, "He's becoming quite a little capitalist."

She made me feel like I had been doing a radio commercial for the corporate life. She had said it as though it was a kind of joke that I was supposed to think was cute. The truth was she was knocking my ideas about getting a job because she was afraid I would become independent. I knew, deep down, she didn't want me to be a success at anything that looked like it might be halfway normal. I was supposed to be a loser like her and Pete. Since she had started it, I didn't see why I should let her get away with it. "So, what am I supposed to do, ask the Party for handouts the rest of my life?"

She gave me a look like I was some kind of traitor and changed the subject by asking Pete if he had been getting her mail. Pete answered that it took a while for the censors to read the mail and pass it on to him. I wondered if the Communists had some kind of secret code that they used in their letters. I wouldn't put it past them. Even though Pete and his comrades all thought they were big time, as far as I could tell, none of them had ever planned anything as illegal as a shoplifting spree. If they had, the man would have been down on them like white on rice. Probably half their members were working for the FBI.

Every guy in this room was in here because someone had ratted on him. If you just went and did a crime, and never told anyone, you probably had a good shot at getting away with it. But once you took on a partner, or told someone, your chance of success went way down. When you looked at it that way, practically everyone in here had done his best to end up here.

Even the guards were losers. They might have the power to crush you in here but outside they were nothing. When someone doesn't believe they deserve respect, they come on like gangbusters: the way these guards were behaving. The only real difference between them and the inmates was the uniform.

My neck wasn't hurting as much. But, every once in a while, the room would start swirling. I was beginning to feel like I might throw up. Just thinking about it could make it happen. To stop the spinning, I started writing the alphabet on my leg with my finger under the table.

My mother was saying, "Richie."

She was saying it like she had said it a few times already.

"What?"

"Are you okay?"

You had to hand it to her; after making me go through all this shit now she was going to start worrying about me. It was no use telling her it was too late for that. What made it perfect was that she really was worried about her little baby boy.

"Don't give me that shit," I said.

It didn't matter anymore if everyone in the room could hear how pissed I was. It was the only thing I could do to stop her from trying to turn me into some kind of limp-dick mamma's boy. She knew me well enough to know how I would take the fact that she was trying to coddle me—especially in a place like this—so, in a way, she was asking me to beat up on her. It was what we knew how to do best, and I could feel myself getting into the swing of it.

Pete jumped in with. "Cut it."

He didn't say it loud, but everyone in the room heard him. The others had tried to go back to their conversations but the geek show we were putting on couldn't help but grab their attention. The ringmaster, up there on his platform, was just waiting for his chance to crack the whip.

I wanted to die. The swirling had started up again. Only now I couldn't control it anymore. I stood up. The guard sat up very straight, and for the first time he looked scared. I could feel the vomit coming up, and I headed for the door. Before I got there I heaved. I tried not to get it on anyone, but there was a guy sitting near the door who got some of it on his shoes. For a second no one moved. Then everyone near me backed away and my mother came rushing up. She put her hand on my forehead the way she used to when I was little and threw up.

I bent over and heaved again. My mother was shouting at the guard, telling him he had to let us go to the toilet. I started spitting out little pieces of the peanut butter sandwich I had eaten on the train. I closed my eyes, and when I opened them again, the shiny floor wasn't shiny anymore. My vomit was spread out in a lumpy red and yellow pool that blocked the door.

A guard had come to the door from the other side and he told me to come with him. "Where are you taking him?" my mother screamed.

"Shut up," the platform guard barked, "nothing is going to happen to him."

The guard led me by the arm. His grip was very strong, like he was trying to hurt me. I would have pulled away except that I kind of liked it. The pain was sharp, and it cut through the dullness of my nausea. I had screwed up everyone else's visit but I was glad to be out of that room. I would get cleaned up now, and I promised myself I never would see the inside of a jail again.

Summer

When the summer temperature becomes unbearable in New York City, anyone who is able to leave town does so. There are a number of rural cottages, resorts, and camps surrounding the Metropolitan Area that owe their existence to this annual exodus. One of these summer camps was called WoChiCa. This name, which might be mistaken for a Native American word, was actually an acronym of Workers' Children's Camp. My mother had been hired there as a counselor, and though I was too young to be a regular camper, I was allowed to attend under the convenient fiction that the camp was providing childcare for one of its workers. The real reason we were there was that the Party, which was running the camp, had decided we needed a respite from the pressure cooker that our lives had become.

WoChiCa's culture leaned strongly leftward; every activity, from cleaning the bathrooms to formal camp meetings, reinforced one message. When we sang, *I dreamed I saw Joe Hill last night, alive as you and me*, we learned some history, but we also felt something, and we were moved a step further from flirtations with left politics toward life-long commitments.

As far as I was concerned, attending WoChiCa wasn't just about politics. During my summer there, I learned that being anonymous was not the only way I could avoid becoming a pariah. I discovered that my ability to deflect attention away from myself, honed on weekends in the playgrounds of Bensonhurst and on the streets of Harlem, was an inferior way of surviving. Even though I was younger than the other campers, my age didn't matter. The spirit of friendship was so strong at WoChiCa that no one could feel excluded.

I had already begun to sense this at Downtown Community and the Jefferson School. But at WoChiCa this realization was reinforced twenty-four hours a day, seven days a week. There was no place to hide, and as a result I learned that I could reveal pretty much anything about myself, or my family situation, without fear of being ostracized. This was such a liberating feeling that I lobbied to go to camp every summer after that.

My mother had sensed the beneficial effect that this kind of environment had on me. She began to pull Party strings to see to it that my future summer camp applications were successful. WoChiCa closed after that first summer, but there was another camp called Kinderland that accepted me the following year. Kinderland, though not directly tied to the Party, was definitely left-oriented. The main difference between the two camps was that Kinderland emphasized secular Jewish culture.

Having grown up in Bensonhurst, I was familiar enough with Jewish culture that adjusting was easy. Over the course of the summers that I spent at Kinderland my fluency in *Yiddishkeit* really deepened. If ease of communication is any indication of group affiliation, it was clear that by the time I stopped going to Kinderland, I was about as close to being Jewish and Black as one could get without being fully assimilated. Of course that didn't mean that I would ever be accepted as a member of either group, a condition to which I might have aspired had I not known it was impossible.

I don't think Kinderlanders cared much about racial and ethnic differences. I was not aware that I was being perceived as different, and that was what was wonderful about the place. There were other non-Jews in attendance, some of them black, but Jewish culture was so pervasive at Kinderland that there was no need for cultural aggressiveness. Everyone accepted that attending camp meant participating in Jewish activities. Exactly what these activities meant in the long run, however, never really made it through to me.

Knowing what *treif* or *bubkas* meant was one thing but understanding what it meant to be Jewish—what, for example, the holocaust meant to my Jewish friends—was completely beyond me. I guessed that Black people felt similarly about slavery. These were atrocities that had to be taken personally, and their meaning could only be fully understood if you did take it personally, but I was incapable of doing so.

It wasn't that I couldn't identify with the victims; that was easy for me. The way I saw it, these were human beings who had been victimized; ethnicity and race, while not irrelevant, didn't really matter. Blacks, Jews, the Japanese at Hiroshima, it was all the same to me. Some groups may have suffered more but no group had a corner on being screwed. I knew that this point of view was incomprehensible to many of my friends so I kept my mouth shut. But my eyes remained open, and I saw the way that horrific human behavior manages to distort the perceptions of those who identify too strongly with the victims.

I know that it is important that awareness of these atrocities be kept alive (if for no other reason than that it may help in avoiding a repetition of the barbarism). But I am skeptical of our ability to learn from these horrors. One part of the problem may be that the survivors' identification with the victims distorts their perceptions. Too strong an identification dulls the ability to come to terms with the qualities and insecurities that have motivated the perpetrators. Dismissing the perpetrators as evil people may provide psychological comfort but it does nothing to produce an approach that disarms future perpetrators.

In creating an environment of mutual cultural trust, the campers and staff at Kinderland managed to come very close to dealing reasonably with one of the great tragedies of the twentieth century. Those of us who were not Jewish had an opportunity to learn about the past, and to share our feelings of sorrow, without becoming defensive. If I couldn't understand exactly what it meant to be Jewish, I did come to understand a lot more about what it meant to be human.

Despite this, for many years I harbored misgivings about Germans. It wasn't until very late in life that I had the opportunity to establish a close relationship with some Germans who had been born in the post-war period. It took some time, but eventually I became convinced that they had managed to see as clearly as one possibly could into the abyss that was their culture during the war, and to come away with an awareness that neither overwhelmed them with guilt nor created a need to project blame on others. This required a finely tuned cultural sensitivity that was manifest in the delicate way they approached all social relations. And that was why they had become my close friends.

The Mayor of 18ᵗʰ Avenue

I had been cutting my classes so regularly that the risk of getting caught leaving GW during school hours no longer gave me a rush. Once you were so far behind in a class that you had no hope of catching up it didn't make any sense to attend and I had reached that point in most of my classes. Some mornings I would leave home as though I was going to school, and I would go to a coffee shop or walk around until the poolroom opened and then I would spend the day hanging out. On other days I would crash one of the movies in Times Square. The theaters couldn't have strong locks on the emergency exits so it was a piece of cake to pop the lock and grab a seat before an usher saw you.

I had already seen all the movies, and I was too broke for the poolroom. I hadn't been in touch with my old man for some time so I got the bright idea of taking a subway ride over to Bensonhurst and checking him out. He went to work in the late afternoon and I knew exactly where to find him before work.

Sure enough, as I was walking up 18ᵗʰ Avenue, I had no trouble picking him out of the crowd of losers hanging out in front of the candy store where they made book. I didn't know any of the guys he was with. When he saw me he didn't try to break away from them or introduce me; he just let me walk up like I was a stranger asking for directions. I stopped about five feet away. His gumbas were staring at me like they thought I was looking for trouble. Finally, he asked me if I had just come from school. The question really wasn't meant for me; it was his way of telling the others that he knew me. On the Avenue a guy wasn't supposed to act like anything really mattered. If I told him I just saw his mother fall off a building, he would have nodded and asked me which building.

His cronies looked surprised when he started talking. They obviously hadn't guessed who I was. My old man had been hanging out on the Avenue every day for so many years that Uncle Georgie had started calling him the Mayor of 18th Avenue. Yet these guys, who saw him everyday, didn't know who I was. Though that may seem strange, it wasn't hard to explain: they never talked about anything that wasn't day to day, like which horse looked good in the scratch sheet and crap like that.

I tried not to let my fear that they had heard rumors about me keep me from acting casual. As long as I could make it seem that my being there was the most natural thing in the world, my old man would be able to carry on without losing face. There was no underestimating his habits: he would have let Adolph Hitler come over to greet him if it could be accomplished without changing the way his gumbas felt about him. This was his whole life, and the last thing I wanted to do was screw it up for him.

I nodded as if to say I had just left school, and he touched my cheek with his knuckle and just held his hand there for a second. He wouldn't want to risk showing any more emotion than this in front of his buddies. They had probably seen him touch every lamppost on the Avenue a million times, and though he was giving me a different kind of touch, they could chalk it up to being the same kind of thing.

Touching me that way was so *him* that, when I rolled my eyes, they all cracked up. Then I told him that he didn't have to worry because I had already finished my homework. The lie was just to keep us from getting into hot water in front of his friends. I didn't know if they had realized that I should have been in school but going into it, at that moment, wouldn't have been the best idea in the world. If he knew what I was up to, he didn't let on; he just asked if I was going to play some basketball. He said it in a way that let his friends know that I was good at the sport. Then, without waiting for my answer, he introduced his friends. "Willie, Barney, Tommy ..." He stopped for a second then continued. "This is Richie."

Willie reached out a hand to shake, and as my hand reached out for his, he shot a lightning left toward my face, stopping as he touched my cheek. I never saw it coming. If I hadn't already guessed from his looks, his move made it clear he was a prizefighter, and an amazing one at that. Then we shook hands. By this time they all must have guessed that I was my father's son. I could see, in their faces, how much they wanted to like me. My father, for all his weirdness, was a stand-up guy, and they were his friends. They didn't care if he touched doorknobs and lampposts; each of them probably did something at least as weird. If I kept my mouth shut, and didn't go into anything important, they would accept me, even though, as far as they knew, I could have just dropped in from Mars.

My father said he would walk me over to Aunt Mary's. He made it seem like it was a plan we had already worked out. Willie tapped me on the shoulder and Barney said, "Take it easy." They seemed eager to push my father along, probably because they were a little uncomfortable being out of their usual bullshit routine.

We walked without speaking for some time. I really didn't have much to say, and I was pretty sure nothing had happened in his life that we could talk about. Walking in silence was probably as good as it could get. Once we were off the Avenue he asked me why I wasn't in school. Alone with him I wasn't about to lie: if he had been a violent man, I'm pretty sure he would have hit me right then and there. I told him I hadn't said anything about cutting school because he was with his friends.

He said he didn't like lies. But the way he said it let me know he appreciated what I had done. Then he asked if *they* had been picking on me. I was surprised; I hadn't figured he would want to go into a subject like this with me. Even if it had been true, there was nothing he could have done about it. He wasn't about to tell me I could come and live with him in Brooklyn. I told him nobody picked on me. I wasn't bragging; it was the truth. There were plenty of guys around who were tougher than me, but except for that thing with the twins, which was ancient history, if anyone was doing the picking it was me.

"So you're making trouble yourself?"

I had forgotten how smart he was. He wasn't going to let me have it both ways. There was nothing I could say, now, that wouldn't lead to things getting worse, so I just kept walking with my mouth shut. It took me a whole block before it dawned on me that my coming there had shaken him up. He was worried about me and wanted to help. There was only one thing he could do for me: so I told him I could use a fin. He reached into his pocket and pulled out a bill. He didn't need to look at it to know what denomination it was. It would be just like him to have different bills in each pocket so he could pull one out without having to reveal his whole roll on the street.

We had made a complete U and we were back on 18th, a few blocks from where we started. I stopped in front of the BMT entrance. He handed me a token. I wanted to give him a hug but I wasn't sure if he would want me to do that here on the Avenue. Instead, I thanked him for the money and he said, "Be careful," and that was that.

On the train ride back to Manhattan, it occurred to me that people always know more about you than you are aware of having revealed: your posture, facial expression, tone of voice, the way you frame what you say, all that and more, reveal information about what is going on with you. Even the best actor can't control it all. My old man knew my whole story, and there was nothing he could do about it.

The train was crossing the bridge into

Manhattan, and I was beginning to feel a little dizzy. As I looked down, I felt as though the train was about to tumble into the East River. I closed my eyes to keep things from spinning, and I didn't open them again until I was sure that we were safely back underground.

Adrift without a flotation device

When I was a kid in Brooklyn there was a crazy man who lived across the street. Every once in a while he would go off his rocker and stand out in front of his house and start screaming. Whenever I heard him, I would crack the blinds to peek out at him. Even though the crack was almost invisible, I was terrified that he would notice and come and get me. His screaming was different from the kind of screaming that went on in our house. He wasn't yelling at any particular person, at least not anyone that I could see, and there was so much anger behind his shouting that I believed, perhaps rightly, that he was capable of doing serious harm.

This introduction to mental illness influenced my thoughts for many years. My first, and usually dominant reaction was one of fear. Whatever was going on with crazy people was mysterious and fraught with danger. It was so different from the way I thought that I just couldn't get a handle on it. Yet, lurking on the periphery was a doubt: what if I was insane?

No one in the entire United States came even close to sharing my experience. Though I sometimes felt like I belonged somewhere, at least when I was at summer camp, the truth was that I had no good friend, or relative, that I could trust with my innermost thoughts. I was alone.

If Pete had been my father I probably would have become a Communist. There were things about the Party you had to admire. Poor people needed a tough bunch of guys to fight for them, and that was what the Party did. But Pete wasn't my old man, and as much as I respected how far he had travelled to make it as a political leader, he had a side of him that turned me off. He was a bully. Though he never pulled his act on me, I had seen him in action pushing people around in meetings. He was capable of throwing a fit that would intimidate even the toughest Communist.

If I had been his son, I might have learned to do that. I certainly was insecure enough to jump at the chance to control people. But I wasn't his son and I didn't identify with him. I had met him when I already had a few ideas of my own, and I resented the fact that he had taken over my life by marrying my mother. Through observing Pete, I had seen what it meant to be in the Party: it was all about discipline, not just the obvious kind (being able to hold your liquor or whatever), being in the Party demanded mental discipline. Your mind had to lock itself into the Party's program. It wasn't just the literal political plan (the flip-flopping, top down, group consensus) that you had to agree with; you had to close off consideration of all peripheral possibilities.

My mind was out there bobbing and weaving in space, and that was where I wanted it to be. Sometimes I acted in a way that made people think I was a fool. But that was just a protective front; I wanted to know everything, the whole ball of wax. In my most buoyant moments I believed myself capable of understanding it all: science, art, philosophy—you name it; I felt I could conquer it.

The other side of that was my awareness that I was adrift without a flotation device: a very scary proposition. I had mastered the art of invisibility; I could walk into a room full of black people and be unobtrusive. I could be far more hidden than any other white person could have been, and I was learning to do this in other environments as well. This required an extremely malleable ego: one that could sense the perceptions of others and shape itself in conformity with the least obtrusive identity that was expected in the situation.

My disappearing act wasn't a particularly good idea, but I was so traumatized by the events that had created my need for it that I couldn't ask myself what I was ashamed of. And having no one who could serve as a model for my identity, I didn't have a clue about who I was. I knew I needed help; if some therapist had thrown me a lifeline, I would have grabbed it. The problem was that therapy was a no-no in the world I inhabited.

From the 1930's to the early 50's most American psychotherapists were left-leaning liberals. There were two distinct approaches: one preferred physiological and behavioral techniques; the other approach focused on insight into interactional patterns. During this time many Communists participated in well-attended public debates on these issues. But, once the government prosecutions of

Communists began, the Party, fearing that therapy might lead to damaging leaks, barred its members from participating in any form of psychotherapy. The Party had a program of *criticism/self-criticism* that served as an alternative to psychotherapy. This amounted to a form of group therapy in which the individual's personal problems were considered in light of the likely political consequences.

Even if I had been a Party member this approach would not have worked for me: I was already far too cynical about the process. While I thought of myself as unique, what I was experiencing was probably a fairly common adolescent crisis. Most people manage to survive these conflicts without therapy, and I did as well. But, having no models or guides to help me shape the adult identity that was trying to emerge, I remained confused about who I was. Around this time I began to see myself as a person who was capable of extraordinary vision, able to see beyond the categories that other people seemed to need. Part fantasy, part reality, this strange self-aggrandizing idea began to take root in my consciousness.

My mother was probably aware of how confused I was. While I seemed to be carrying on in a tradition she favored, that of committed radical, it was fairly obvious that I was also a poolroom hustler with a strong need for immediate gratification. I was dangling between dogmatist and downward-spiraling hipster, and there was little that anyone could do about it. In some other family, a therapist or a cop would have been called.

NY, NY to LA LA

Pete had been a Party organizer on the West Coast before coming to the National Office in New York. He still had many contacts in California, so it was decided that he should move there when he got out of jail. I never learned who made the decision; my best guess is my mother, through Pete, had something to do with sending the idea up the Party's chain of command. No matter who authorized the move, the fact is it changed my life.

The Party had agreed to help us get settled, and Pete was to join us when he got out. When my mother told me we were going to move to California, my first thought was that I wouldn't go. It didn't take me long, however, to see that remaining in New York, on my own, wasn't realistic. Though nothing had been officially recorded, George Washington High School and I had pretty much come to the end of our relationship without the requisite graduation. My mother had pressured someone into getting me hired as an office boy for the Civil Rights Congress but that job hadn't lasted, and there were no legitimate jobs on the horizon. Because I thought of myself as some kind of hustler, it was pretty clear that if I remained in New York it wouldn't be long before I was into very deep water of some sort.

By the time the train pulled in to Union Station in Los Angeles, I was pretty sure that moving to California was the right thing to do. Everyone knew that California wasn't rigged the way New York was: you had a better shot at creating a reasonable life there. Though I missed my friends (I was sure that anyone I might meet in LA was going to be a hayseed or a rube) the future seemed to be open in a way that it could never be for me in New York.

The party assigned a white guy to help us find a place to live. He picked us up in a car and told us that we wouldn't have any trouble finding a house to rent until we were ready to buy. I figured the Party had given us a complete flake. How were we going to rent a whole house, much less buy one?

He explained that Los Angeles was actually a bunch of small cities clustered around the city core like pieces in a jigsaw puzzle. He told us that Mexicans lived East of the center. My mother wanted to know if they were descendants of the original settlers. He answered her quickly, explaining that most of the people living in East L.A. were recent immigrants from Mexico; many of them weren't citizens so they were easily exploited. He went on to say that Negroes lived in an area that ran south from downtown, and in a strip that ran west. Homes had been bombed, and people had been shot when Negroes first moved in to some of these areas but nothing like that had happened recently.

I was beginning to think he wasn't as flaky as I had thought. He was telling us all this to help us understand where it would be best for us to live but he wasn't making the decision for us. Like me, my mother had taken him for being a little slow; she had been flattering him. Now, though, I knew she was beginning to trust him. She told him she thought it would be best to start looking in one of the transitional neighborhoods. He handed her a newspaper, and she started reading the street addresses out loud. If he didn't know a particular address he would look it up on the map. She circled the affordable ads that were in the right neighborhoods.

We stayed at a motel for a few nights and then we rented a house, a whole house, near the intersection of La Brea and Adams. It was close to two bus lines: one that ran East-West and the other North-South. The house had a yard in front and one in back and it was separated from the neighbors on both sides by a narrow walkway. It was even partially furnished with a stove, refrigerator, and washing machine. All this rented for less that we had paid for our New York rat-trap. To cap off our good luck, my mother found a job as a bookkeeper. When she promised to support me as long as I stayed in school, I told her I would do my best to graduate.

After all this good luck I expected Rose to brighten up a little but she still didn't seem very happy. When I asked her about it, she said happiness wasn't the most important thing in life. Then she went into a routine about how much suffering there was in the world and how it didn't have to be that way. I told her that when you got a break it didn't help to worry about people who were down on their luck because there was never enough good luck to go around, and if you worried about them you would never stop worrying.

What I had said was true. There aren't many opportunities in life to experience joy. My mother didn't drink or use drugs. She had no sexual or creative outlet, no way escaping thoughts about pain and suffering. She had abandoned a religion that provided a way of interpreting suffering, and she had adopted a substitute that proclaimed an end to it once the revolution was accomplished. But, until the revolution came, pain was all there was. She wasn't exactly depressed: Rose was outer directed; she didn't lie around the house in her bathrobe moaning all day, but she was never truly happy. Though I was sorry for her, I made up my mind I would never cut a path for myself that made it impossible to experience joy, at least once in a while. I was already well on my way to becoming a true Californian.

The Alexanders

I missed Manhattan, mess that it was, and as yet Los Angeles had proven to be a big zero. The palm trees had taken over. You could walk the city streets for an hour and never run into anyone. If by some miracle you did see someone you knew, when you asked what was happening they would say, *"You got it my man."* People talked like their brains were clogged. White people would pick up right away that I was from New York. My Harlem way of talking, which I never used around white people, didn't fit in either; black people had a more southern drawl. It was as if all of California, white and black, was a record running at slow speed.

Our first friends were the Alexanders. They lived in a house that was a mess: the paint was peeling, the screen on the front door was torn, and some of the boards on the porch gave when you stepped on them. The only thing growing in their yard was a palm tree that looked like a big skinny pineapple. If it wasn't the most beat up house in the neighborhood, it had definitely made it to the semi-finals.

These Alexanders were even stranger than we were. In the time that I knew them I had never heard anyone one say the father's real name. Everyone in the family, including his wife Mimi, called him Daddy. Friends called him Alex. He had been a hod-carrier before his back gave out, and he was still active in the union. Even though he wasn't working—I guess out of habit—he would go down to the hiring hall in the morning. He would be back around noon with a bunch of the guys who hadn't gotten work that day. They would all hang out on the front porch playing dominoes and shooting the breeze until dinnertime.

The wife, Mimi, was white. She was tiny, and she always spoke in a whisper with a southern accent. Her daughter, Gail, who seemed to be white too, was even quieter. She was about my age and either very shy or retarded; she never said enough for me to be sure which it was. The rest of the family all seemed to be Daddy's children: Gus, whom I never met and Don were adults; Charlene and Hardy were young adults, and then came my friend Franklin. Finally there was the youngest: Stanley. All of the children, except Gail, were dark: none of them seemed to be the child of both Mimi and Daddy but the truth is, I had no idea who was whose child. No one ever said anything about it and I never asked; we all kind of liked it that way.

My mother had met Mimi and Alex through the Party. She brought me over and introduced me to Franklin. He asked if I played basketball and that was it. We went over to the park, played a few games, and by the end of the day we were good friends. He may have been told the story of our family, or he may have guessed from the way I spoke; in any case, he treated me like I was a long lost cousin.

Even though the difference would have been obvious to anyone who wasn't blind, all their friends, and everyone in the family, treated the Alexander progeny as if each was the birth child of Mimi and Alex. Everyone in the family spoke with a similar accent. It wasn't exactly Southern; it was more like a kind of black down-home, *sure I sound simple, so simple you understand me perfectly*, way of talking. Charlene was the exception; she had a very soft, polite manner; she never raised her voice in an exaggerated way. Their way of communicating was very good for letting you know how they were feeling, a kind of safety valve for emotions. I was beginning to learn how to talk trash with them and I was enjoying the hell out of being part of their program.

Gail had the most low-key way of talking. Sometimes I got the feeling she made herself sound this way so that no one would get the idea that she thought of herself as better than the others. We all respected her for that but the problem was that she had gone way overboard. It didn't matter why she did it, or how it started, for better or worse, *timid* was the name of Gail's game. She had mastered the disappearing act.

Don, lived across the street. He had done time for strong-armed robbery and, as far as I could tell, now that he was out, he was up to his old tricks. His sister, Hardy, was even closer to the edge than he was. Every so often she would go into a complete laughing fit over something that might not have been worth even a little lightweight smile. There was a strong sexual edge to her; she always seemed to be inviting excitement. Don and Hardy didn't ask for trouble, no more than a firecracker asks for a match.

It was hot, and I had come over to the Alexanders to see if Franklin wanted to go to the beach. Everyone in the family, except Don, was out on the porch when I got there. Daddy and his crew from the Union were running off at the mouth and slamming tiles as usual. On top of that Bessie Smith was blaring on the record player, hollering for pig feet and a bottle of beer. I jumped right into the middle of it, running my mouth to beat the band. It was like the fourth of July out there on that porch, we were all having a hell of a time.

A police car, cruising the neighborhood, pulled up in front of the house. Something I had never seen before happened: the domino game came to a complete standstill. Nobody on the block was uptight enough to have called the police; they probably were drawn by the commotion—God forbid that some people could be enjoying themselves. These L.A. cops were different from the police in New York. Neither of these cops had one hair out of place. In weather like this a New York cop would have his shirt open, and you would have seen sweat running down his back. All these guys did was ride around in patrol cars all day with the air conditioner on and the windows rolled up. They didn't look like they even knew how to sweat.

The normal way to act, in this kind of situation, would be to cool it. But the Alexanders were not normal. We all knew Daddy kept guns in the house, and we all knew he wasn't likely to back down from anything. The domino game started up again; the players were slamming tiles like the cops weren't there. We were all thinking the same thing: *get your clean-cut ass out of my face.*

It hadn't taken me long, after we moved to Harlem, to learn that, when a cop is on a street in a poor neighborhood, everyone knows about it in no time at all. I looked across the street; there was Don leaning back from his window so you could barely see the top of his head. Then he disappeared, and I knew he was going for his gun. Hardy went inside; a moment later Bessie Smith's volume went up a few notches. It was like Bessie was here with us, acting her bad-assed self, daring the cops to make a move. I was getting very scared. These cops didn't have a clue about what they were getting into. I could see where they might get off a shot or two in our direction before Don started firing. When that happened Daddy would break out the guns, and the crossfire would start. Of course that wouldn't be the end of it. There would be other cops, and the shooting would go on until we were all dead.

One by one we went inside. Only the domino players and Daddy remained on the porch. These guys from the hiring hall were tough; I wouldn't have been surprised if more than one gun was being readied at the domino table. I very much wanted not to be there. But, like it or not, I was part of this family now. I admired the way everyone was acting. They all were displaying an, *I'm not going to take no shit,* attitude. This was especially true of Daddy. He wasn't jumping bad with the cop, just the opposite, he got up from the table and stood by the front door like a man waiting for the mail to be handed to him.

Both cops got out of the car; the driver stayed by his door. The other cop started to walk toward the porch. I think he realized, by how calm Daddy was being, just how much trouble he was in. Without making a big deal of it, he unsnapped the leather strap that held down his pistol. He did it very casually, like he was scratching himself. As soon as his partner saw this, he leaned back into the car and picked up the microphone to radio for help. I figured Don wasn't going to let that call go out.

I had heard it said that the LAPD recruited cops in the South. As far as I could tell that was true: I hadn't seen very many black faces in their cars. My guess was most of them were good old boys who didn't think very highly of people like us. I had been concentrating so hard on what was going on outside that I didn't notice that Mimi had gone over to the record player. A moment later the music stopped right in the middle of one of Bessie's lines. When that happened the cop seemed to relax a little. The head of the one who had gone for the radio popped back up over the roof of the car again. Don's head appeared in the window. He had a funny look on his face, like he couldn't figure out what was going on. Everything froze for a second and then the cop started walking forward again. When he got to the porch stair, a voice rang out: "That's far enough."

It was Daddy. His voice made it clear the cop had done something wrong. The main problem was the way the cop was walking. His head had been moving from side to side. He was taking his own good time coming forward, acting like he owned the house and the whole damned neighborhood. After Daddy spoke, the cop just stood there staring straight into Daddy's eyes. Even though he had to look up to Daddy, he didn't seem to be one bit intimidated. It was like he was glad someone had come forward, like we were just a bunch of rowdy kids and Daddy, old as he was, was the ringleader. I guess he figured he had someone he could use as an example to the rest of us. He had no way of knowing how wrong he was. He was dealing with a tight family; even the domino players were part of us now, and each of us was ready to die for the others.

Daddy asked what the cop wanted. The cop didn't answer, instead he had a question of his own: "Do you live here?"

Daddy said, "Damned right I live here. Now what the hell do you want?"

The cop turned to his car and nodded. His partner started to lean into the car again to make the call, but before he got the mike to his mouth, Mimi went out to the porch. Both cops' heads snapped up at the sight of her. Neither of them moved. Mimi, in her quiet voice, said, "Is there a problem officer?"

The cop standing at the bottom of the stairs kept his attitude: you could see it in the way he was pushing his chest out, but his voice didn't have the same anger in it when he answered. "It's the noise."

"We'll keep it down," Mimi said.

The cop decided to speak politely now. "Please see that you do."

He looked from Mimi to Daddy, as if Daddy was her kid and she was supposed to control him.

Then, before anyone had a chance to say anything else, he turned and slowly walked back to his car. I was still wondering if Daddy was going to let him get away with that attitude when the cop reached his car. Then the cop turned and paused, as if he was giving us time to come back at him. Finally, he got in and they pulled off very slowly. They had figured out exactly where the edge was and now they were walking it.

Once they were out of sight no one said anything for a long time. Then Mimi came inside and the men got back to their dominos. As Bessie's song started up again I heard one of them say, "That cop's ass was lucky. She put his head back on straight."

Now, many years later, I know how things turned out for some of the members of this family. I don't know what happened to Mimi, Daddy, Gus, Don, Gail or Stanley. The last thing I heard about Hardy was that she was in prison for bank robbery. Franklin committed suicide in middle age. The collapse of Communism in Russia brought about a split in the U.S. Communist Party. Charlene became the head of the Committees of Correspondence, one of two branches in that split.

The Prom

Dorsey was the high school nearest to where we lived. It was located between white, black, and Japanese neighborhoods. That made it one of the few somewhat integrated schools in the city. I didn't know any whites there but I had met a few of the Japanese students. They called themselves *Buddha-heads* and they hung out in a bowling alley near school. *Buddha-head* was probably originally a derogatory term that these very tough guys had turned inside out. One day one of my friends, a guy named Myron, who had been dissed by one of the white football coaches, went after the coach with a length of chain. Myron was literally half the size of the coach but the coach didn't feel superior; he turned tail and started running.

As usual, the only people I got to know slightly well were black. On weekends our favorite place to go was Sugar Hill. Most of the houses in that neighborhood were large and owned by successful Negroes. There were several black frat houses there that usually partied on Friday or Saturday night. The uninvited would wait outside until a large group had assembled and then we would all rush the door at the same time. Once inside, I would wander around listening to the music and occasionally dancing. I thought I was a pretty good dancer; I could shimmy when I did the Hully Gully better than most guys. Usually the rooms where the dancing was held were dark enough for me to blend in without calling too much attention to myself. I suppose the idea was to meet someone, but I was never successful at that.

Once it started getting late we usually cruised around the city in someone's car. L.A. was all about the automobile. Soon after my mother arrived she bought an old Nash Rambler convertible. A day or two after she had acquired it, I was driving. Sugar Hill was near the Western Avenue strip between Adams and Washington Boulevards. This was the street-walking capitol of L.A. The women who plied their trade on Western Avenue knew we didn't have any money, and they generally ignored us. Among my friends it was a mark of pride to announce that you would *never pay for it*. I subscribed to that view but, like them, I couldn't help cruising Western late at night. The scene was too full of sexual charge for a guy my age to resist.

Like any street savvy New Yorker I had learned to monitor body language. You could sense when something was happening on a street: everyone's attention would begin to focus in the same direction. It was like watching a flight of birds, each bird would be picking up cues from the others, and then, all at once, the entire group would shift direction. If you watch people you learn that, before all else, the eyes give away where attention is being paid.

Being street savvy in L.A. was a little different. First of all, people in L.A. didn't make use of the sidewalk. You might cross a sidewalk, once in a while, to get to your car, but that was about it. Once the bars closed, however, the sidewalks along the Western Avenue strip came alive. The women of the night were out there making eye contact with men in the passing cars. And in the cars that cruised the Avenue, all eyes were focused in the same direction. Meager as this voyeurism was, it was as close as I got to sexual activity during my high school years.

During the one year that I spent at Dorsey High I didn't learn much of what they were teaching. But that didn't seem to matter: the fact that I showed up, and didn't cause any major problems, apparently was all that the school authorities needed to move me through the system. I was approved for graduation, and like everyone else around me, I was faced with the question of what to do about the Prom.

I hadn't exchanged more than a few words with any girl at the school. The few girls who had smiled at me were all black. I didn't have nerve enough to ask any of them to go with me, and even if I did get up the courage to ask, and they said yes, the thought of integrating the Prom scared the shit out of me. Technically, the Prom was integrated: any student could attend. But the fact was that blacks took black dates, Japanese took Japanese, and whites took whites.

I wasn't afraid of physical violence. There were a few white jocks tough enough to start something but everyone knew the black guys would finish it, and they would be on my side. The real problem for me was the need to overcome my natural partiality for anonymity.

There was one girl I secretly admired. Though

I had only exchanged looks and a few words with her, I was sure that she liked me. I stalled about asking her, and before I could get up the courage, someone else asked her. When word got out that she had accepted I was devastated. After that I gave up hope. Then, in a casual conversation, a girl I hardly knew brought up the subject. Before I could really consider what I was saying, I had asked her.

The Prom was held at someplace called the Deauville Club out at the beach. I picked her up, gave her the obligatory corsage, and we drove out there. It was very awkward. All night I felt like there was a spotlight following us around. Fortunately, we managed to muddle through the entire evening without a serious mishap. The pressure we were under was so intense that, if we had been lovers, we would have been bound to one another for life.

As things were, however, all I could manage was a peck on her cheek at the end of the evening. Being in *like* is not being in *love*. We were both strongly aware of that. I wasn't sure of her motivation; she seemed as confused as I was. The only strong emotion that I felt—other than relief at the event being over—was guilt. I had been so stilted and uptight all evening that I was sure that I had come across as angry and uninterested in her. I was certain that I had managed to ruin one of the most important evenings in her life.

The Draft

As my eighteenth birthday approached I started getting nervous about registering for the draft. I had thought about becoming a conscientious objector; the problem was that you had to belong to some organized religion to receive CO status. It appeared that atheists, or agnostics who leaned toward atheism like me, didn't have enough moral standing with draft boards to be granted CO status.

I could have joined a church that sheltered COs but that would hardly have been an act of moral courage. In addition to being an agnostic, I wasn't a pacifist; I believed in self-defense. What I objected to was the American military; I believed the war machine acted primarily in the interests of the wealthy and powerful. Though it was called the Defense Department the fact was that the military was oriented toward fighting abroad. I knew that if a war did break out I might be ordered to kill a foreigner on his own soil, and that was something I wasn't prepared to do. I knew there would be serious consequences if I disobeyed once I had been inducted.

I thought about not registering, but it seemed to me that doing so would haunt me as long as I lived. It wasn't realistic to think that you could live a whole life without having some governmentally sanctioned identity. I consulted an attorney named Frank Pistana who had been recommended by my mother.

Pistana promised to help me with free legal services no matter what I chose to do. It was pretty clear to me that my only options were jail or Canada. I decided that I would register and go through the process until I was sure I was about to be arrested, and then I would head for Canada and try to make a new life.

My pre-induction physical wasn't until 1963 (I was twenty-three at the time). By then there were 16,000 American troops in Vietnam but the U.S. involvement hadn't begun to reach the levels it did later. Since my local board was in central L.A., the men who showed up for their physicals with me were almost all from poor families. Most of them were Hispanic or black, and no one seemed to be well educated. When the moment for induction came, I was supposed to swear allegiance; instead I quietly, with my heart pounding, stated that I was refusing to do so.

The guy who was running the show acted as though I was some kind of comedian or wise guy. He appeared to be very angry. He lectured me, in front of the others, on the seriousness of what I had done, and he threatened me with jail. He was clearly unprepared for my refusal. In the entire country at that time, there were probably no more than a handful of men who had done what I had just done. When I didn't try to argue with him or offer any explanation for my behavior he put me in a room and let me watch the clock for several hours.

I guessed he was checking with his superiors, and I wondered how far up the chain the whole situation had to go before he got his answer. Eventually he came into the room and told me that I could leave and that there would be an investigation. I don't remember being told who would be conducting the investigation.

Later I learned, from a neighbor, that there had been people going around in the neighborhood asking questions about me. Other than that, I heard nothing from the Army or the FBI. As the war in Vietnam heated up, large numbers of young men faced a similar situation and resistance to the draft increased. By that time I was student, and miraculously when I applied for deferments I received them.

I don't know who was involved in reviewing my draft status, or what led to my being allowed the various deferments. If I were commanding an army the last person I would want in the ranks was someone with a history of not running with the crowd. That may, or may not, have been the reason for my good luck. In any case, I managed to get through the entire Vietnam era without having to leave the country or go to jail. As usual I was not about to ask any questions that might call attention to me. If they wanted to make believe I didn't exist that was fine with me. I did, however, confront the war machine, anonymously, on the streets at just about every demonstration that was held in my vicinity.

My lucky day

After graduating from Dorsey, I was sure I was finished with school forever until I looked around for something to do with my life. Since no realistic future life called out to me I did what many of my fellow graduates were doing: I enrolled in a Junior College. The State of California was engaged in a great democratic experiment. The Junior Colleges were tuition free institutions that enrolled just about anyone who applied. As far as I could tell they were not all that different from High School. The major difference, it seemed to me at the time, was that they allowed card playing in the cafeteria.

I had already been playing there long enough to be known as the white whistologist. I was good, but by no means the best. My partners and I might win a few games, and then the cards wouldn't be there, and we would have to sit out a few games. One day I was dealt a perfect hand. Etiquette calls for laying down the hand before play begins, but I was so full of excitement that I wanted to stretch out the experience as long as I could. I played each trick as though I wasn't sure of the outcome. When my partner figured out that we were unstoppable, he played joyfully. Neither of us hid our pleasure as we slammed down each card.

I held back an ace until the last trick to make it

more exciting. When I played the ace my partner jumped up, and as our opponents tried to slink away, we made so much noise that everyone in the cafeteria noticed. Normally at this hour there would have been another team ready to play, but none of the usual players was around. I asked my partner why the place was almost empty and he said that he thought people might be at the rally.

At Dorsey High School there had been events called PEP rallies. Though PEP probably had some other meaning, to me it meant energy. That fit with what these rallies did; they built up the crowd's energy and enthusiasm for a sporting event. To my way of thinking a person was either enthusiastic about something or not, getting together in a crowd to change how you felt didn't seem to be a reasonable thing to do. Though the idea was ridiculous, there were a lot of students who seemed to think milling around and cheering for the home team made sense.

But I wasn't aware that any games were scheduled. When I asked about this, my partner looked around uncomfortably and said, "It's about what's going on down South. You know, that segregation shit." I suggested that we check it out but he said he had to get home so I wandered around until I noticed a crowd that had gathered near the Vermont Avenue entrance to the campus. Half a dozen people were standing, with their backs toward Vermont Avenue, facing a crowd of about fifty people. One person was addressing the crowd.

He was speaking in a quiet voice; if I was going to be able to hear what he had to say I would have to squeeze into the crowd. That didn't appeal to me: if anything happened I would be stuck, unable to move quickly. So I walked around the edge of the crowd and out onto the sidewalk. From there I could hear without being trapped. I noticed an older guy with a camera circling the crowd. He didn't look like he was from the school paper, though I couldn't be sure, Los Angeles City College had a lot of older students. He was taking shots of people in the crowd. I turned away when he tried to take a picture of me.

At the back of the crowd there were four or five white guys bunched together in a little gang. They all had crew cuts. I was on the basketball squad, and I hadn't noticed them in the gym so I guessed they were would-be jocks. They were clowning around but not doing any serious disrupting. I figured that, in a crunch, only a couple of them would want to fight. Not that the rally supporters looked like they were big time brawlers. I did see two guys I knew from whist. They would hold their own; so if the organizers didn't panic, the crew cuts probably wouldn't be able to break up the rally.

The guy giving the speech held up one finger, like he was about to make some important point, but no words came out. He just stood there with his mouth open, looking like Sid Caesar doing his German professor routine. Then he keeled forward and fell on his face. I couldn't tell whether he was joking or he actually passed out. Everyone moved forward to look at him, and a couple of the organizers bent down to check him out.

People started pushing. Now, I was very glad I

wasn't in the middle because it looked like people were going to get trampled. A couple of the crew cuts moved forward, and one of them stepped on a girl that had fallen. She screamed and the guy who was with her started wrestling with the crew cut guy. Someone shouted for everyone to sit down. One person sat, and then another. Soon there was a group seated around the speaker who was still down. Now that people could see what was happening the panic subsided. The wrestlers were separated. A guy with a guitar started singing, *"Oh Mary don't you weep, don't you morn,"* and others joined in.

The words of the song are spoken to Mary, mother of Jesus. They tell her not to weep because Moses parted the Red Sea and drowned the Pharaoh's army. The basic idea is that miracles are supposed to make you feel good about something bad that has happened. Taking pleasure in all those people drowning didn't seem to me to be something a good Christian should be doing. Still, the singing did calm people down. People were swaying in time to the music. Then the speaker got up on his feet, just like Lasarus, and everyone cheered. He held up his hands, everyone quieted, and he started talking again

"Some of you may have heard that students in the South are being arrested. All they were asking for was the right to be served. Some of them have been beaten. They need our help. Students all over the country will be protesting. We are going to boycott Woolworth stores because they have segregated lunch counters in the South. This Saturday we will have a picket line at the downtown Woolworth store.

Please join us."

People began to cheer again. Then the crowd started breaking up. The guys with crew cuts left, and so did most of the rest of the crowd. The few people who remained stood in little clumps talking quietly. No one was arguing. There were some good-looking women hanging around, and it was pretty obvious some of the guys were using this as an excuse to get to know them. But most of the people who remained didn't seem to be thinking about that. I was excited by the thought that I might meet some white people my age who were aware that the whole world wasn't white. I went up to the speaker and asked him for a leaflet. He handed me one and asked if I needed a ride to the demonstration. I said I would get there on my own. Then I told him I thought that what they were doing was great.

Picketing 1960

As I walked up the block toward the Woolworth store I had to restrain myself from lurching forward every few steps. I was excited: I had never heard of picketing for something like this. There was no telling what might happen. Anything was possible; we could be beaten, thrown in jail, or worse. I couldn't help thinking one or more of us might not survive the experience. If there were cops in the area, they were doing a very good job of keeping out of sight. In any case, I didn't expect that they would be protecting us; if anything they would be kicking ass.

It wasn't just fear that was making me break into these little jogs. I was about to meet people who were willing to put their lives on the line for something everyone else was trying to ignore. Even if they didn't know what they were getting into—some of them probably felt the cops would protect them—I still had to respect them for what they were trying to do.

Everyone in the little group huddled together out in front of the store seemed as anxious as I was. I recognized several people from the LACC rally. I did my best to control my body as I walked up to them; the last thing I wanted was for them to think I wasn't cool. The thing was: I was already beginning to feel like I didn't belong. They seemed to know one another and they looked at me anxiously, as though I might be there to harm them. Most of them dressed like they were dirt poor. Any fool could tell they had money. From the way the guy had spoken at the rally, it was clear he had grown up in a family that was college educated.

The demonstration had been scheduled to start at noon. It was already half past twelve and nothing was happening. Because I was terrified, I yelled, "I was at the City rally. Any of you mind if I start?" I had gone overboard to impress them, but no one reacted. Now, my supposedly confident ass had no choice but to pick up a sign and start picketing. The signs were in a neat stack at the curb. I picked one up, hooked it over my shoulder like a rifle, I started to pace in front of the store. My heart was pounding. I could feel their eyes on me. Even though the energy was just bursting out of me, I made myself walk slowly. When I reached the end of the store, I turned. Several of them had fallen in behind me.

By the time I made a full circle everyone in the group was picketing. I couldn't help notice one girl in particular. She was holding her sign the way I held mine. As she walked toward me she gave me this really intense look. She had curly hair and milk-white skin and I could see, right away, how it would be with her. After a while some other people joined the line and she moved just behind me. She asked my name; after I told her, she said her name was Susie Fefferman.

Having a conversation with her over my shoulder was just fine with me. I always feel a little phony making eye contact with people. The idea that you can tell if someone is speaking the truth if they look you in the eye is ridiculous, and trying to seem sincere by making eye contact was a manipulation I couldn't bring myself to engage in.

Susie told me she had heard about the demonstration from friends at school. She was very straightforward when she talked. There was none of the cynical edge that New York girls had. After a while she was walking next to me. Every once in a while she would look over at me and her face would light up. I was laying it on: not using words so much as just letting her know with my body that she was wanted.

A guy appeared out of nowhere. Before I knew what was happening he was up in my face shouting. "Nigger lover." He was bigger than me. From the way his thick neck disappeared into the top of his jacket I knew he could take me without half trying. It was the kind of move that never should have happened. If I hadn't been so busy sweet talking Susie, I would have made him, and I would have prepared myself, long before he could have gotten this close. But now he was right up on me, and my body was not ready.

He spit at me. Luckily, he missed. Then he backed up like he was waiting for me to come at him. That was his mistake. He was too big to mess around with. I reached my arm back to the top of my picket sign and grabbed it like a spear. I figured that if I could take out an eye, I might keep him from doing serious damage to me.

Just as I was about to bring my arm forward one of our guys stepped between us. He said. "Don't do it. He wants you to fight." *NO SHIT*, I thought, but I was stuck; if I tried to push our guy aside I would be off balance and Mr. No Neck would have an edge on me. There would be no way I could inflict any real damage. Our guy put his arms around me and said, "Don't you get it. If you fight with him, the police can come in here and haul us all away."

I knew he was right. But I also knew that it wasn't just the logic of his argument that was keeping me from going after No Neck. Fear had taken over. Our guy was giving me some bullshit about "passive resistance" and all I was thinking about was how I could hurt the asshole without getting seriously injured myself. Our guy was providing me with an out and the coward in me took it.

Our picket line had come to a dead stop. Out of the corner of my eye I could see some guys inside the store laughing and pointing at me. I held up my sign and started walking again. An old lady in our line turned to me and said, "He whose food I eat, his song I sing."

It sounded like something out of the bible, but she was right: a minute later the guys inside the store came out and joined the jerk. Every time I would pass they would give me hard looks but they didn't make any moves. They just stood there making wisecracks. Inside the store there was a guy in a suit shrugging and making faces like there was something wrong with us.

Then one of our guys started singing. He had a deep voice, and he just let three words out, slow and steady: *We shall overcome*. After he sang it through he added: *someday*. The song was so easy to sing, everyone in our group picked up on it. Even though I can't carry a tune, I joined in. We sang it through a few times and then we change the line: *We are not afraid; we are not afraid, today.*

I couldn't believe what was happening. People were leaving the store empty handed. What was more, the fact that I hadn't hit the guy made me score even bigger with Susie. She had taken to holding my hand. Most of my life I had felt it would be great if you didn't have to fight but, before this, I had never met people who actually believed it. The picketing, the singing, the laying it on the line for non-violence created a feeling of great strength. You couldn't help feeling it. By the time we had gone through a few more verses, everyone—even the jerks hassling us—understood we couldn't be stopped. A guy parked his car, got out, and joined the line. Then, as though someone had turned on a tap, people started coming out of nowhere and picking up signs.

I was beginning to feel as though I had stumbled into the middle of some religious experience until I looked in Susie's eyes. Her focus was pretty intense, but it was not of the spirit. The manager put a *CLOSED* sign on the door and started letting his employees out. Three of them, all women, walked away in a group, each of them staring down at the sidewalk and not saying a word. Then a black woman, looking like she was about to croak, dashed out of the store and hurried down the block. After that the guys who had been hassling us took off too. Once they were out of sight we all started cheering, and the picket line collapsed.

Now we were just a crowd of excited people shaking hands and laughing. People were trying to decide where the party would be. Everything was happening at once, the guy who had kept me from hitting the jerk volunteered his house, I was asking Susie for a ride, and she was hugging me.

Her car turned out to be a Studebaker. I had never liked the way the Studebaker hood came to a point in front. It was a hokey design that repeated itself in the trunk, so you almost couldn't tell which way the damned car was headed. Susie's model, though, was the exception. It had two doors, not the usual four, and instead of coming to a point, the hood and trunk were flat. There was one straight line from headlight to tailfin on each side of the car. You could almost see how smoothly the air would flow over the car.

She unlocked it like she had no idea how classy it was. The whole deal didn't make sense: she didn't seem like the type to be interested in cars, yet to get a model like this you had to go through some serious car hunting. As I got in, I asked her where she got it. She said her father had given it to her for getting good grades. When I asked her where she went to school, she told me she went to Fairfax. Now I knew two new things about her: she was a good student, Fairfax wasn't an easy place to get good grades, and she was probably Jewish.

She pulled out of the parking space and asked if I was from New York. My accent, as usual, had given me away. I said I was, and she asked, "What part?" I told her Bensonhurst and Harlem. If I had just said Manhattan she might have let go of it. But I had opened the door, so she pushed her way in: *"Isn't that a Negro neighborhood?"*

Her eyes were off the road, and on me, and she was making it pretty clear that if I didn't talk, she was ready to grill me. I figured I might as well cough up the whole story. When I finished with my mother and Pete she said, "So that explains your accent."

It was the right thing to say. She hadn't even hinted that my life was weird. If she had started showing that she pitied me, I would have told her to pull over. Instead, she had just made a sensible observation about where I had lived and how I had grown up. Her reaction made me want to tell her more and so I did. Pretty soon I was piling it on pretty thick, and she seemed impressed. She seemed at ease with me and she told me a little about herself. Her mother had grown up in a small town where there weren't many Jews. Her mother had come to L.A. to go to college; she had met Susie's father, and she never graduated. Now, her mother kept the books for the family business. Her old man had grown up in Boyle Heights. At the time it had been a Jewish neighborhood. His parents had died when he was young, and he never finished Junior High School. By the time her father was in his twenties he was running a successful printing business. Now he was in real estate.

She didn't have to add that real estate had been good to him. I could tell that she was embarrassed by how much money they had. She hadn't turned down the car, so she wasn't *that* embarrassed. I had just snagged a part-time job in a trophy store doing specialty printing. After I told her about it, I realized that I sounded like I was comparing myself to her old man, so I changed the subject by asking her what she did for fun. She told me she played the guitar and went to hoots.

I wasn't exactly sure what a hoot was, but I knew it was very square. She explained that they were held in coffee houses and they sang folk songs. Whatever it was, it wasn't something I planned on doing, so I asked her if she liked to dance. It was a stupid question. Even if she liked to dance, there way no way she would know how to dance. Her idea of dancing would be the Lindy, or something like that, where the guy throws the girl around a lot. I had noticed, the few times that she walked in front of me on the picket line, that her spine was too tight. As hard and unnatural as it is to make your hips move forward and back when you walked; that was what she had done. I knew we wouldn't hit off on the dance floor.

She said she wasn't very popular at school dances. To me, she was just about perfect in every way. But the chumps at her school wouldn't know enough to appreciate her. They would have gone for big tits and straight blond hair attached to a girl who spent her whole life putting on make-up. Susie didn't wear any make-up at all.

It had been nice to be able to tell her about Harlem and not to have to worry about her thinking I was some kind of freak. I knew it made me interesting in her eyes, and I was glad for that, but the reputation I would have in her crowd wasn't going to be easy to live with. I didn't want to end up like some football hero who has to play the big game over, and over, for the rest of his life.

There was something else bothering me too. The one thing I knew for sure was that I liked being outside the general program. Not going along with the crowd was the best thing I had going for me: it meant I could slip in and out of places most people didn't even know existed. But here I was: letting a straight girl—one I hardly knew—get a good idea of what made me tick. I was just a short step away from being part of her straight crowd. Hanging out with people who got picked up by daddy whenever they stumbled was bound to turn you into a pretty useless individual. It wouldn't be long before I would be taking stuff for granted the way they did, and I would start believing in the correctness of the general bullshit.

Elsie and Louis

I could hear people talking but I couldn't make out what was being said. It occurred to me that I was sleeping in a new place. I hadn't been living with Rose and Pete for weeks. Since I didn't have a place of my own, every new morning brought with it the challenge of figuring out where I was. As soon as that problem was solved, I would start thinking about where I would be sleeping that night. Finding a place to stay would have been much more difficult were it not for the fact that most of the demonstrators were my age, and many of them were willing to put me up for a night or two. It was pretty clear, however, that some day I would wear out even this very liberal welcome. I didn't have enough money to set myself up in a more permanent living arrangement, so I just took each day as it came and tried not to worry about it.

I had been sleeping with a pillow over my head. When I peeped out from under the pillow, the light was so bright I thought I was sleeping outdoors. With a hand shielding my eyes, I looked around. I was inside some kind of glassed-in room. There were some plants around but not enough for it to be a greenhouse. The place was furnished like a living room. I was on a sofa bed in my underwear. My clothes were on a chair nearby. I grabbed my pants and put them on.

I recognized Susie's voice and remembered

making up the sofa bed the night before. A deep voice was talking over Susie's, as if in another conversation. I guessed it was her father on the phone. This seemed like a good time to make an entrance. The glass room connected with the dining room and off that, through a doorway, I could see a refrigerator. Swallowing my embarrassment, I walked into the kitchen. I was relieved to see that my disheveled appearance matched the informal dress at the table. Both of Susie's parents were in their bathrobes; her father hadn't shaved; her mother's hair was set in a long braid down her back. Susie's father sat opposite the door, his head tilted to one side; he had the phone tucked between his chin and shoulder as he cut himself a piece of cheese.

Susie was pouring coffee for her mother. When she noticed me she said, "Mom and dad this is Richie; Richie: Aaron and Helen." Her father put down his knife and waved a *hello* without losing a beat in his phone conversation. While I was deciding whether or not to shake hands with them, Susie's mother got up and pointed to her chair. Since there were only three chairs in the kitchen, I shook my head and went out and grabbed one from the dining room. The opportunity to demonstrate that I was somewhat civilized relaxed me a little. I sat facing Susie's father. Helen's bathrobe started to slip apart and I had to work hard to keep my eyes on Aaron. Susie was already dressed so there was no danger there. Helen spoke as Susie poured me a cup of coffee.

"Were you comfortable out there?"

Her neck had reddened a bit but her smile,

Susie's smile, never left her lips. Usually when a person smiled for that long I began to sense phoniness, but it wasn't that way with Helen.

"I slept pretty good. That's a really nice room; the light is fantastic. Did you build it yourselves?"

The newspaper, spread out on the table in front of Aaron, was open on the real estate want ads. There were long pencil marks down each column that stopped at three circled ads and then continued.

"We had it done before we moved in. It's best in the afternoon when the sun is going down. Sometimes we have drinks out there at the end of the day."

I was glad, very glad, that I was speaking with Helen. Though I wasn't following what Susie's father was saying on the phone—it was about some deal—I could tell he was doing a pretty good job of intimidating the person on the other end of the conversation. Neither of Susie's parents seemed to be put out in the slightest by my being there. Having a guy pop out of the sunroom to join them for breakfast couldn't have been a common occurrence, but they were doing a great job of treating it as a regular part of their morning routine.

I asked Susie how she had slept, and she answered by saying that her bedroom was on the other side of the house and didn't get as much light when the sun came up. Now that her mother had been informed that I hadn't been in her bedroom, I relaxed. I was trying to think of a question that would let me know what Susie had told her parents when Helen spoke.

"Susie told us that you two met at a demonstration. Do you think they are having some effect?"

I didn't want to get into a confrontation with them. But, from the way she spoke, it was pretty clear she was sympathetic.

"If it was just happening in the South, the Woolworth people might be able to hold out. But we're really hurting them up here. No one goes in while we are out there. They have to be feeling it."

Helen said, "What you're doing is very important."

She sure knew how to make you feel good. I tried a little modesty: "The brave people are the ones in the South."

My nervousness returned as I noticed Aaron hanging up the phone.

Helen continued. "Yes, that's right. But I'm really proud of what Susie, and you, and the others are..." Aaron interrupted. "And the poor schmucks who work there and are laid-off are proud too."

Aaron's tone made it clear that he wanted to steam-roll the conversation but Helen answered calmly. "I'm sure Richard understands that."

"So his understanding makes it OK to interfere in a local business that doesn't segregate?"

I couldn't tell if he was serious. Susie said, "Daddy," in a voice that gave it away.

I tried to match Aaron's commanding tone as best I could. My voice was way too high, but I made it sound tough. "It's not local, and besides we're not trying to interfere, we're trying to shut them down."

Aaron seemed to enjoy that; he changed his tone. "They'll come around. Publicly held retail operations are very vulnerable. Stockholders get very nervous when people stop buying."

I was impressed. I hadn't given a thought to how the actual decision would be made, it required the kind of economic knowledge that was beyond me. I knew enough, though, to respect the practical nature of Aaron's thinking. I also knew the mechanics didn't matter all that much. I agreed. "That's for sure: when we show up only air will be coming in and out of that store. Sooner or later they are going to buckle."

A bell rang. No one moved to answer the door. By way of explanation Susie said, "That's Elsie."

I heard the front door close and a few seconds later a black woman came into the kitchen. As she took off her coat Susie introduced us. Elsie put her coat on the counter near the sink and poured herself a cup of coffee. Aaron asked her how Louis was doing. She replied that he was feeling much better and that he had gone around back to start on the sewer line. Then she put her coat over her arm, and with the cup in her other hand, she left the kitchen, saying that she would start in Susie's bedroom.

Before Elsie was out of earshot Susie began explaining that Louis was Elsie's husband and that both of them had been working for the Feffermans for a long time. I asked Aaron if he was in the real estate business, and he said that he preferred to call it the search and rescue business. Then he asked me what I did. I told him I was a student at City College and that I was working my way through school. He asked where I worked and I had to admit that I was between jobs.

Helen interrupted the inquisition by observing that Louis might be able to use some help. She explained that he was digging a ditch in the backyard to replace a sewer line. Aaron gave Helen a look that didn't hide the fact that he was annoyed at the bind she had put him in. But the flash of anger disappeared almost immediately. It was clear that he was used to acceding to Helen's demands. I could almost feel the pleasure he took in complying with her wishes. I realized his capitulations had a practical effect: reluctant consent allowed him to keep up the ogre act without provoking a real confrontation. I was beginning to like the guy.

He answered by stressing that digging a ditch was hard work, as if he was trying to convince me not to take the job. We both knew that was a hopeless gesture. So he simply took me out to the backyard in his bathrobe and slippers and introduced me to Louis. When I shook Louis' hand it was like squeezing a piece of concrete. Louis gestured to a point near the house and drew a line with his finger describing the path of the sewer line. Aaron said that I should do the digging, and Louis should do the supervising.

Louis looked me up and down and said, "I guess he might do. Ever done any digging?"

I didn't want him to think I was some rich kid out on a lark so I said, "Hey, digging is my middle name. No way I can't handle a small job like this."

Aaron shook his head at this and said to Louis that he shouldn't let me fall asleep out here. They both laughed, and Aaron went back to the breakfast table. After Louis showed me what needed to be done, and gave me a pick, I started swinging it to beat the band. I was a little hung over so it was hard to keep going, but I knew a chance like this didn't come along everyday so I pushed myself until Louis said I should take a break. It turned out he was a great guy to work for: he didn't give me a hard time, but he made sure the work got done. Elsie brought us sandwiches, and the three of us ate at a picnic table in the backyard. Though I brought up Aaron's toughness neither of them said anything negative about him. It was clear that they both trusted him, and that made me feel that I hadn't made a mistake in not setting my salary before starting on the job. I knew I could trust that it would work itself out. After all, Aaron trusted me with his daughter: for all he knew I already had knocked her up.

The situation of these two families reminded me of a book I had read, *Like One of the Family*, by Alice Childress. In it, a day worker is talking to her friend Marge about her job cleaning white people's houses. In one vignette she confronts her employer who is explaining to a friend that she is like one of the family. She makes it very clear that her life is very different from that of her employer. There is an edge to Childress' character that I couldn't detect in Louis and Elsie. Part of the difference, I was sure, had to do with the fact that Helen and Aaron didn't patronize these two people who worked for them. Elsie and

Louis, for their part, kept a dignified distance from the Feffermans. Both families were friendly; they could laugh together and display affection for one another, without becoming saccharine or fawning.

The men's roles were very clearly defined. Aaron was the boss who gave assignments to an experienced and talented employee. Though Aaron was a formidable intimidator, there was no bullying of Louis: Aaron understood the limits of what Louis would tolerate; and as far as I could tell, those limits allowed Louis to retain his dignity. The relationship between the two women was less clearly defined and more complicated. Both women were very generous with their emotions and neither woman seemed to harbor resentments or significant prejudices. If Elsie coveted Helen's affluence, it was never apparent to me. Elsie seemed to have a realistic appraisal of the economic gulf that separated them. Although I couldn't be sure, it was my belief that she didn't see Helen as someone who was exploiting her. If anything, she saw Helen for the generous person she was.

The relations between the sexes also weren't strained. There was no sexual charge between Elsie and Aaron that I could discover. There may have been occasional moments of frisson between Helen and Louis. They were both far more attractive than their spouses. But they were both in control of their impulses and neither would have seriously considered rocking the boat. Good humor and sensitivity seemed to prevail across gender lines.

It seemed to me, the relationship between

these two couples was very rare. There may have been other interracial relationships like this but they must have been few and far between. This was not paternalism, nor was it full equality; it was two relatively enlightened families in an economically and socially skewed relationship making the best of it.

TB

I was crashing wherever I could, sleeping, whenever I couldn't find someplace else, at Susie's. The Feffermans were incredibly generous. They never seemed to mind finding me in the sunroom when they woke up. I didn't want to wear out my welcome so I tried not to overdo it. I kept most of my clothes at my mother's house in Altadena. Pete had contracted TB in jail, and since TB patients couldn't sleep in the same area with uninfected people, the Party bought them a cottage in Altadena that had an in-law apartment carved out of the garage.

Pasadena was a short drive, by Southern California standards, from downtown L.A. In the fifties the black population of the town had grown rapidly, and toward the end of the decade, nearby Altadena was beginning to become integrated. I had managed to put together enough money to buy an old Ford, and from time to time, I would drive up there to see Rose, Pete, and the boys. Visiting them was also my chance to exchange the dirty clothes in the car's trunk for a clean set that my mother had washed.

As soon as I opened the front door, I could hear his cough. Even a cursory glance at Pete was enough for anyone to see that he wasn't well. He had lost a lot of weight since entering jail, and his eyes had sunk back in their sockets. He moved slowly, as though the energy had been sapped out of him. As I shook his hand I tried to let the expression on my face communicate that I was glad to see him. He smiled at me and said I looked great.

I couldn't help thinking that the government had really done a job on him. None of it was an accident. This was exactly what you got when you went up against something that big. No one person had brought him down. No one had issued an order, or lifted a finger. Pete had tried to stop a bulldozer with his bare hands, one way or another he was going to get badly hurt.

It didn't take long for the conversation to get around to his illness. He wanted to go to the Soviet Union for treatment. I knew if he went over there he wouldn't come back. He was trying to get Rose to come with him but she wanted to remain in the states with the boys. It made sense for him to go. They would take good care of him, and he wouldn't have to worry about the treatments being appropriate. He would get the best medical care they had. I didn't know if their doctors were any good but they would surely pay attention to him. Except for a few Party doctors, who probably weren't specialists in TB, that wasn't going to happen in America.

Pete included me in the idea. He seemed to think we all would have a jolly time over there. I got off the hook immediately by telling him I wanted to stay involved in the Civil Rights movement. That excuse trumped everything. Pete, and Communists generally, were delighted with the movement. As far as I could tell just about everyone in the Party, in

Southern California anyway, was involved in the movement in some capacity. But the Party people kept a very low profile. They felt, rightly, that any open involvement would retard rather than enhance the movement's progress. In any case, it was pretty obvious to me that the Communist Party was history. They still had some influence in a few unions but none of the big moves were happening at their behest. Pete was one of the Party's top leaders on the "Negro Question," and he could leave the country without it making a bit of difference.

Of all the reasons people married, love was the only reason that could come close to explaining a choice that had made their lives so difficult. What Rose was facing now wasn't just another difficult choice; this one was impossible. Pete would be better off in Russia, but if she went with him she would have to keep her mouth shut for his sake. What about the boys? She was stuck. I knew she was beginning to have reservations about the Party, but she and Pete were dependent on it for his survival. Being separated from Pete, again, was going to be very painful especially since she would be forced to choose it herself. I really felt sorry for her.

Charles White

Charles White, an artist, lived near Pete and Rose. He was a leftist in an interracial marriage so it was natural that he would be close to my family. Sometimes, when I was in Altadena, I would visit him. He was a light-skinned black man with short, neatly trimmed hair. He dressed casually and carefully: maybe a shirt with a collar, a muted V-neck sweater, chinos, and penny loafers. Though he wore thick lenses in heavy frames, you didn't get the impression his vision was restricted; his glasses made him seem focused. If it weren't for the glasses, and a couple of moles on his face, you would say he was handsome.

Charlie always seemed relaxed and confident. Somehow he managed to be self-assured without becoming arrogant. His wife, Fran, was about his height and weight; and like him, she was cordial and tranquil. They both seemed in good shape physically as well. She didn't wear much make-up. She looked like a fresh, clean-scrubbed, mid-western farm girl. Both of them were friendly, but not in some do-gooder, *isn't civil rights wonderful*, way. I didn't think Charlie earned a lot of money from his art. Fran had a job and they lived comfortably. They didn't own anything that looked really expensive but it wouldn't have been like them to show off their money if they had it.

Usually, soon after I arrived, Charlie would

take me through the house to his studio where the walls were lined with drawings of black people. These charcoals had been done fast and with very sure lines. The subjects were regular, everyday people. You could feel the power in their muscles and the joy in their movements. His drawings reminded me of Nat King Cole's singing; it made you feel that the act of creation was the most easy, natural thing in the world.

One of his paintings always got my attention. It was of four people: an automobile mechanic, a longshoreman and two big women in print dresses. They were standing around in a circle facing one another. The women were in the center of the canvas and you could see more of them. The only color in the whole painting was in the women's dresses. The result was that the dresses seemed super-real; they just popped-out at you, and the women, because of this, felt very earthy. Everything Charlie did was a celebration of the human body. For the most part his subjects were sensible, robust people. Occasionally a very delicate figure would be depicted.

Charlie's enchantment with the human body was a remarkable recreation of Renaissance form in modern social dress. It was clear that he understood exactly where he stood in the art world. He was aware that Altadena was not New York, and Social Realism (even with a black twist) was not Abstract Expressionism. Yet there was no evidence of jealousy or outrage at the way his talent and skill had been relegated to the periphery by the collectors. The fact that he was able to remain steady and non-polemical was a tribute to his finely tuned artistic temperament.

I was in awe of his talent and amazed that he and Fran had managed to create such an uncomplicated life in the shadow of his prodigious gifts. It was hard to understand how this had come about. No doubt their temperaments had something to do with it. Charlie was just too shy to dominate a room and too fair-minded to let people put themselves out for him, and Fran, somehow, managed to let his work take first place in her life without becoming a martyr to it. She seemed to have no interest in guarding his time or making him seem special.

Whenever I entered Charlie's studio I felt a little guilty about having interrupted his work. That feeling usually didn't last because he would simply continue with what he had been doing. We might not talk for minutes at a time, and that would be fine. Then I would get a bright idea and open up the conversation. Mostly we talked about art.

I remember saying once that I thought art was different from everything else in the world because it always worked on more than one level. He gave me a little smile that told me he figured I had said a mouthful, and then he acted like he had to think about it. He leaned forward so that his nose was practically up against the canvas. I always sat facing him so I wouldn't have to look over his shoulder. Usually I didn't care about the details of what he was doing on the canvas, but right then I was curious about what he was staring at. But I didn't peek, and finally he spoke without looking away from his work.

"What makes you think there's only one level for everything else?"

I had already prepared for that question, so I answered quickly. "I figure science is supposed to account for the rest of it, and science acts like there is only one level."

"Have you ever heard of wave and particle physics, Richie?"

I didn't have a clue as to where he was headed, but he didn't wait for me to answer. "When physicists try to describe the way the atom behaves they use two different models. Sometimes they assume the atom acts one way and sometimes the other."

He didn't have me yet. "I suppose one guy is looking at it one way because he's trying to solve one kind of problem, and the other guy, with a different problem to solve, sees it differently. But the world doesn't have a problem to solve; it just is. It's just there in its one and only way."

I figured we were headed back to the usual tree falling in the forest thing but he was ready for me.

"Let's try it this way: you, Richie, a real person, are sitting in front of me, no?"

Just to be difficult I said, "How do you know that?"

"That's not relevant. You're just clouding the issue."

"Okay, I'm sitting in front of you."

"Good, now the *you*—sitting here—isn't just one thing: there's your body, your mind and everything in it: dreams, memories, whatnot, and then there's your jive: all this bullshit you're trying to lay on me. There's no one *you*; you're nothing but a bunch of *yous*, and one of you better stop giving me this lame argument."

I laughed but I wasn't going to let him off the hook that easily. "Okay, you take your Jackson Pollack. Now the man throws a can of paint on his canvas. Is that art?"

"Yes, it is."

He had answered very quickly, as if he didn't care that I might be leading him into one of my traps. That was fine with me. "Okay, how do you know his work is art?"

"It's done in a context—part of which includes the work of other artists—and it's done for an artistic purpose."

I figured I had him now: "How do you know what his purpose is?"

He hesitated a second before answering. "From viewing his work."

I shouted: "So the work speaks to you. How come the world doesn't do that?"

Charlie said, "Have you ever seen a sunset?"

"Damned right I've seen the sun set and it didn't say bubkas."

"Was it beautiful?"

"Not like a painting."

I loved this. I had him back-pedaling now. He even looked away from his work. It felt right to be telling this artist that art was more important than nature, or reality, or whatever the hell we were talking about. And, Charlie, in telling me it was no big deal, was doing something he felt good about too. Though we were yelling at each other, we were both happy. I had known, all along, how much he respected the part of the world that wasn't art. It was obvious in every carefully produced brush stroke he made. But I wasn't about to say that.

Helen and Aaron

Most of the people that I met at the demonstrations were college students. Hanging out with them, I began to spend more time studying. My grades improved and, by the time I finished my AA degree, I was able to switch to Los Angeles State College. My living arrangement stabilized too. Without anyone seeming to notice, I went from accepting an occasional dinner invitation to sleeping over regularly at Susie's. Helen, more than anyone, was responsible for this. It didn't take her long to start acting as though I was a close relative, not a member of the immediate family, but not just another guest in their household.

It was impossible not to like Helen; she was a warm sun in the Fefferman family. Aaron was the cold moon. He had only one soft spot in his rock-hard shell: every once in a while, he would shower Susie or Helen with baby talk, or he would snuggle up to one of them as if he was a newborn baby searching for a tit. This was so unlike him that I was sure that if he ever did it to me, I would go into immediate cardiac arrest.

He was always fair with me but he never let me lose sight of the fact that he was paying all the bills. I tolerated his abrasiveness; any response in kind would have made a mess of the otherwise reasonable life I had stumbled into. It wasn't just a desire for comfort that kept me in line. I was making love to his daughter and that gave me a feeling of power over him.

There was another reason he didn't get to me. There was a buffer: Susie's brother Danny. He was a musically talented kid who was just setting out on a journey that would take him into the drug world and from there into the orbit of the Moonies. Aaron wasn't any harder on Danny than anyone else Aaron dealt with. That was the problem: since it was either Aaron's way or the highway, Danny didn't have much room for personal growth. Helen did her best to run interference for him but there were inevitable clashes. Danny's struggle to get free of his overbearing father pushed him into a rejection of everything his parents valued. In the process he came to accept the discipline of an even more authoritarian figure: Mr. Moon.

It was pretty clear that Susie was turned on by the fact that I wasn't like all the guys she had grown up with. The upper middle class just didn't produce an Aaron or a Richie. This fact accounted for a good deal of the sexual heat between Susie and me. I was playing someone I had been, not the person I was becoming, but I wasn't about to abandon the role. Given the situation I had no incentive to ditch my street-tough front. Even Aaron respected me for not letting go of who I had been.

Since I had no previous experience with people who were wealthy, my first impression of the Feffermans was that they were rich. Once I got to know them well, it was clear that my initial impression had been inaccurate. They had enough money to live very comfortably. They probably could have acquired a house in Beverly Hills, but they preferred the slightly downscale Wilshire District. Unlike the Hollywood wealthy, Aaron had no need to impress people with his money. He had other uses for it. The only exception to that was the brand new Cadillac he bought every year. That, like everything else about him, gave away where he had come from. Every other material thing, thanks to Helen's taste, played down the money they had. Of course very little of it was in cash; it was all invested in real estate.

Their furniture was modern; the tables, chairs, and sofas, were all simple designs. Helen's taste wasn't exceptional. One of the few oils she had acquired—an abstract seascape in red, painted by Polia Pillen, a well though of local potter—was displayed prominently. None of the art was extreme, really expensive, or deliberately challenging. The current *New Yorker* was usually on the coffee table. I started reading it at their house. In those days I found the whole gestalt—a magazine for people who considered themselves sophisticated—infuriating.

I often disagreed with the Feffermans on most of the subjects that interested me and I thoroughly enjoyed arguing with them. They had a circle of friends who would come over for drinks. Most of these people were successful professionals. Unlike Aaron, they had attended college. Some of them had grown up with Aaron, others were people Helen had met through her political and social-philanthropic activities. Most of their friends were liberal and Jewish, and every one of them, sooner or later, became involved in some real estate deal Aaron had cooked up.

I didn't understand the details of these deals but the basic idea was that they kept income from being taxed. These deals would allow a loss to be declared while the properties were actually increasing in value. As far as I could tell, it was a shell game that was completely legal as long as the money kept circulating.

Aaron must have benefited from investing their money. At the very least he had more financial leverage than he could have mustered on his own. But I don't think that was the only reason he did it. He liked being around these successful people, and he especially liked the fact that they trusted him and relied on his guidance. He was outspoken and rough, but they didn't seem to mind, and I guessed it wasn't just because he made money for them. Aaron enjoyed deflating pretension, and he was great at cutting through a puffed up argument. He was respected for this, and this respect gave him great pleasure.

Several times a week a group of their friends would gather in the Fefferman sunroom or, if the occasion happened to be a bit less intimate, the Feffermans would entertain in the living room. Aaron or Helen would serve drinks to everyone, including Susie and me, and we would all shoot the breeze about the topic of the moment. My ideas were always treated with respect, even though I was by far the most radical person in the group. If there was condescension, it was so subtle I wasn't aware of it. The only time I felt I needed to proceed carefully was when race came up.

I hadn't told anyone except Susie about my family background. I guessed she had told her mother, and Helen had probably told Aaron. But their friends had no way of knowing that race was a subject I couldn't take lightly. Fortunately, none of their friends was an out-and-out racist. But I was pretty sure that each of them assumed he or she was better, and smarter, than any black person. That may explain why there were no black people in their social crowd.

It wasn't hard to understand how they had come to see themselves as superior. I had just been helping Louis remodel one of Aaron's apartment buildings. Aaron asked Louis to install a sink on a particular wall. Louis, who could keep a diagram of every pipe in the Empire State building in his head, immediately saw that it would be too expensive to locate the sink where Aaron wanted it. Instead of telling Aaron his plan was a mistake, Louis asked him where the feeder pipe was. This led to a discussion of options; by the time the agreement for the new location of the sink was agreed upon Aaron was congratulating himself on having been smart enough to avoid a costly mistake. Everyday experiences like this inevitably produced a sense of superiority in the person with power.

This event was on my mind when Helen started reading an article to the drinks group about a sleep-in that was going on in a new housing development. The developer was refusing to sell a house to a Negro physicist. I decided to make my feelings known before it was too late. "That's outrageous, if the man has the money, the law should see to it that he can buy any damned house he wants."

I figured that putting the *damned* in there would signal how strongly I felt. Aaron, who was mixing drinks, shouted. "You can't force a seller to take any offer. Where do you draw the line? If Louis offers me two grand for this house, should I have to take it?"

One of the guests was a judge. He said, "It all comes down to the reason for the refusal. If the seller indicates he wont sell because he doesn't like the buyer's race, then, depending on the jurisdiction, it may be illegal."

Aaron shot back. "What if I happen to like your race, but your race is going to lower the value of my property?

That was my cue. I wasn't sure how serious Aaron was but I figured it was time to fish or cut bait. "That's where we come in. That sleep-in is making sure that if that physicist can't buy there, no one else will."

Susie chimed in. "Would you like to come out there with us daddy?"

Aaron smiled at Susie. "No thanks, darling, we have other plans for the evening. That reminds me, where are we eating?"

Helen said, "I thought we would try that new fish place in Playa Del Ray. I've made a reservation."

Aaron loved to fish, and he began listing the types of fish that were in season. Everyone seemed happy with the turn the conversation had taken. A few minutes later they had all drained their drinks, and they left for the restaurant.

The Festival and the party

I've always been uncomfortable with the idea of grooming. Though I associate it with snobbery (horses and dressage) that's not what really bothers me. It's the groomer's conscious shaping and manipulation of how a person is perceived that I can't stand. Grooming is a violation of a person's natural being. Though much of it is innocuous, a face-lift doesn't really bother me, some of it is deadly serious. It wasn't until I attended the World Youth Festival in the summer of 1962 that I understood that the shaping of a person's self image was a much more profound form of grooming. Those of us who attended the festival were being groomed for roles in Communist movements. It wasn't our appearance that was being manipulated; it was our actual being: who we thought we were. Though I partook of the events, in the end, I left the bride waiting at the altar.

About six months before the festival began I learned that a committee was being formed to organize a contingent that would travel from L.A. to Helsinki where the festival was being held. I knew several people who planned to attend an organizing meeting, and when they invited me to go with them, I went. I was beginning to think of myself as a good orator so I volunteered to be a speaker at fundraising events. Eventually I raised enough money to be given a scholarship that would pay my airfare to Luxemburg. From there I hitchhiked and took trains to the site of the festival.

I had expected a lot of pageantry, which always turned me off, so I wasn't ready for actually being moved by the events. It wasn't as though the spectacles changed any of my core beliefs; the events were too ephemeral for that, but I definitely had the feeling that I was part of a very large movement. There were many delegates from poor and undeveloped nations, large contingents from a variety of racial and ethnic groups. It was thrilling for me to think that we all shared the same goals of liberation and equality. Now, having the benefit of greater distance from these events, I am aware of how misleading my feelings were. At the time, though I hadn't lost my critical faculties entirely, I couldn't help being drawn into the strong current that drove this overwhelming feeling of unity and purpose.

Near the end of the festival activities, I was invited to travel, expense free, to the Soviet Union and Eastern Europe. At the time the State Department discouraged travel in the Soviet orbit and few Americans had travelled there. Despite my worry that I might lose my passport when I returned to the States, I was enough of a schnorrer to accept the offer.

The trip was a barely disguised effort to recruit people who were sympathetic toward the Party but were not yet members. At first I was surprised at how skeptical some of the people in our group were. It wasn't until I realized that we were all involved in protest movements that I understood why this was the case. If we were rubbing against the grain at home, wasn't it likely that some of us wouldn't gladly put on a different straight jacket abroad? Not everyone was critical of the dog and pony show the Russians were putting on for us; there were plenty of true believers in the group.

That some of us could maintain distance was all the more remarkable given the extent of the effort being rolled out for us. We were hosted at receptions by the mayors of major cities, given excellent accommodations, taken on tours of factories and museums, plied with alcohol and food, transported in relative luxury from place to place in the Soviet Union and Eastern Europe, and generally treated as very important people. While none of the receptions, lectures, and discussions presented us with information that was critical of Soviet style socialism, it wasn't hard to read between the lines.

The art we were shown was primarily socialist realism. In one museum, when I asked about the impressionists, I was taken to a corridor where major works, collected before the revolution and immediately after it, were on display. The other galleries were crowded but no one ventured into this section. Was it possible that Moscow's museum visitors didn't see any value in this remarkable collection of impressionist and post impressionist art?

I didn't think anyone was monitoring the traffic in and out of this section so there were few risks involved for anyone who might want to view this art. I concluded, sadly, that this art was seen as decadent. Though the true believers used the term regularly, decadence in art was a concept I had difficulty grasping. The closest I could come to it was when I thought of how I viewed some of the minor artists of the Rococo period. But that was kitsch; it might be aesthetically repulsive to me but I didn't consider it dangerous in the way a Stalinist might have viewed the work of Magritte or Duchamp.

The cultural gulf was major. We had some avant-garde jazz musicians travelling with us. I had been listening to jazz regularly for years, and it was hard for me to appreciate the "free" jazz they were playing. They were out beyond Monk or even Cecil Taylor. When they performed no one knew what to make of them; there were stunned silences followed by polite applause. No criticism was ever voiced: after all, they were presenting the music of an oppressed group. My guess is the Stalinists thought they were charlatans but it would have been impolitic for them to say so.

It was obvious that we were being shown the most modern factories, with the most up-to-date equipment, but it didn't take an engineer to see that their infrastructure was inferior. Though there were exceptions (the Moscow subway for example) not much of what we saw compared favorably with what was available in the U.S. When one of us would voice this kind of observation we would be reminded of the fact that Soviet Union had been decimated in World War Two. Several decades had elapsed since the war but that didn't seem to count for much with our guides.

Being able to ignore the obvious gives one an

advantage in a bureaucratic environment. While our hosts were familiar with that form of survival, the critics among us operated differently. In addition to the specific questions we had about particular economic practices, there was one general question that loomed ominously: if socialism couldn't benefit the average person what good was it? I bought the argument that in certain areas (for example: medicine and education) the Soviets had made consistent progress. But in other areas (the provision of consumer goods being the primary example) they couldn't come close to being able to compete with capitalist economies.

This problem bothered me but an objection that was raised by some of the people in our group was even more troubling. Most of us had heard rumors of mass persecutions and killings. In 1956, at an extraordinary meeting of the twentieth congress of the Soviet Communist Party, some of the crimes committed during Stalin's regime were publicly revealed.

In general, the apologists in our group felt the charges of genocide were simply anti-communist propaganda. I didn't dismiss these stories as a lie, but I chose not to push harder to learn more about what had taken place. I let my belief in socialism obscure the importance and extent of these atrocities. The grooming had taken its toll; I wasn't about to join the Party, but I didn't challenge our hosts to reveal more about the anti-Semitism, the extent of the terror, or the degree of demoralization and cynicism that had become endemic in Soviet society.

Valentine 1963

I wasn't exactly homeless. I could have lived with my mom and Pete but that appealed to me about as much as trying to sleep at a rock concert. Instead, I bounced around from one friend's couch to another. I knew that this nomadic existence couldn't go on forever. Though the people I had met in the movement were incredibly generous, I was tiring of the role of chronic schnorrer.

Susie and I had been seeing a lot of one another, and as time passed it became obvious to both of us that living together might not be a bad idea. When we heard about a place that was for rent in Echo Park we decided to take a look at it. We were both only half-committed to living together when we drove down the wooded dead-end road called Valentine Street. Fifteen minutes later we had seen enough of the rustic bungalow to decide we had to live there. It was terrific: a split-level on a hillside with a fabulous view that looked out toward the Glendale Hills. It felt more like a country cabin than a house in the middle of a major city. And it was affordable!

When Susie told her parents, they balked at the idea of the two of us living together. They were supporting her, and though I was earning some money, I was indirectly benefiting from their support of her. That was reason enough for me not to want to alienate them. In any case, going against their wishes wasn't something Susie was prepared to do. That didn't mean she couldn't try to bring them around. Fortunately, before anyone else grabbed the bungalow, Helen softened on the idea. She helped us reach an accommodation that would satisfy Aaron: we could live together if we got married.

My attitude toward marriage was similar to the biblical injunction: *Render unto Caesar the things which are Caesar's.* For me, marriage had very little to do with how I felt about Susie. It meant little more than filling out some bureaucratic documents and appearing at City Hall. I knew there were legal consequences, largely of the financial variety, and that didn't concern me in the least. It seemed to me that a coming together of two equals implied that either person was free to redefine the relationship at any time. The reality was that you decided to live with someone and you stuck it out as long as it seemed to be worthwhile. That seemed morally defensible as long as I didn't hold a double standard that required my partner to commit to perpetual fidelity. It was my assumption that Susie felt similarly but the truth is we never really discussed our long-term expectations in a direct way: we wanted the Valentine house - her parents wanted us married - we got married, end of story.

The Movement in Los Angeles

I don't know about what went on in the rest of the country but it was quite clear to me that when the civil rights movement began to take hold in Los Angeles in the late fifties and early sixties it was primarily driven by two groups: church people who were mostly black, and leftists who were mostly white. Both groups were focused on what they saw as the big picture: most of the leftists believed civil rights was just the opening wedge of a movement that would demand complete social and economic equality for everyone. It was an illusion predicated on the assumption that once people were in motion, their momentum would carry them toward greater understanding of the way inequality functioned in the society. It seemed obvious to us that, given America's racist history, an economic system that produced a few big winners and many losers would inevitably produce a black underclass. While it may have been obvious to us, our point of view was never adopted by large segments of the population.

So where did we go wrong? One important development, few of us noted at the time, was a gradual shifting of goals. The initial opposition to segregation was replaced, over time, with a demand for equal opportunity. Segregation was an easy target because it was morally bankrupt: those Klansmen weren't wearing hoods because they felt morally superior. Once those laws and practices started to crumble we could either work for the elimination of poverty or we could demand equal opportunity. The movement, and the country as a whole, embarked on both courses simultaneously. But equal opportunity, though resisted by people with something to lose, was the easier row to hoe.

Had the war on poverty succeeded, the race problem would have disappeared. The actual result however - the relative success of a formal system for dealing with a claim of discrimination and a retreat in the war on poverty - has led to the doubling of blame being heaped upon the victims. Having a level playing field only works if the players are equally skilled. Anyone familiar with our educational system knows that parental income is highly correlated with academic achievement.

Though I was aware of all this at the time, the real choices were either to support a movement headed in a questionable direction, or to be irrelevant. So, I watched as, one by one, former radicals were coopted by the Great Society. Most of us marched forward with tight smiles, aware that the game was over and in winning we had lost. As the Leopard, in the Lampadusa novel, remarks. "It was necessary for things to change in order for them to stay the same."

My FBI file

Here is how my FBI file begins:

"The Bureau files concerning Rizzo and the information furnished in referenced letter indicates that in 1960 Rizzo was vice-chairman of the Independent Student Union (ISU) and was also a guest speaker at a Los Angeles Cultural Club function where he was billed as a ISU leader. It is also noted that he is the stepson of Pettis Perry, who in 1962 was a member of the National Committee, Communist Party USA, and that his mother, Rose Perry, was also active in the Communist Party as late as 1961. Rizzo had also been present, in 1959 and 1960, at functions sponsored by the Southern California District Communist Party which were open to both members and nonmembers of the Communist Party and that he had continued his active participation in the activities of the Citizens Committee to Preserve American Freedoms, the Fair Play for Cuba Committee, the Progressive Youth Organizing Committee and the Los Angeles Festival Committee for the Eighth World Youth Festival.

"Accordingly, the Bureau believes that such activities warrant the inclusion of his name in the Security Index."

My inclusion in the Security Index in 1962 meant that whenever my name came up in connection with any FBI investigation it would be noted in my file. In 1998, I obtained a heavily redacted copy of that rather thick file. Almost all of the information contained in the file, that hadn't been redacted, was public information: either school records or information that I had attended meetings that were open to the public.

My being elected as Vice-chairman of the Independent Student Union apparently tipped the scale enough to get me included in the Index. The file contains a document concerning the purpose of the Independent Student Union:

"We, the members of the ISU, are dedicated to giving our energies to building a world of peace, wherein the peoples of all lands will not have to live in constant fear of nuclear, biological and chemical warfare. We pledge our efforts to ending all social inequality based on race, creed or national origin and to further the eradication of discrimination in all walks of American life. We affirm the right and value of both students and instructors to take an active role in the political life of the nation, and believe that no restriction should be placed upon the free expression of ideas and opinions with and outside the classroom."

Why such innocuous goals delivered me into the hands of the FBI is a question only someone immersed in the history of the period could answer. If these statements reveal anything, they suggest a high level of naiveté. I did believe, and still do believe, in the values underlying these ideas—I was for disarmament, free speech, and against discrimination—but I believed they could not be achieved without a major reorganization of the economic order. Perhaps, in some weird Kafkaesque way, the FBI understood the duplicity involved in sketching such lofty goals, and took that into account when I was placed on the Security Index.

What I didn't understand at the time was that freedom of speech and legal protections against discrimination could be approximated without an economic revolution. In any case, our statement of purpose was an organizing tool. I don't think anyone who was involved in forming the ISU was unaware of this. We were trying to build a student organization that was a radical alternative to the usual sandbox politics that students engaged in at most colleges.

I knew the government had its eye on me. If I hadn't been Pete's stepson there would have been less attention paid to me, but I had called attention to myself with my behavior at the draft board. There was a separate file, referred to in the FBI file, kept by the Department of Defense, and my FBI file also makes it clear that when I was out of the country I was being tracked by an agency that worked out of U.S. Embassies.

None of this really mattered. I was mildly fearful of what might happen to me, and perhaps it affected my behavior in ways that I am not aware, but what I did was determined more by my natural predisposition toward keeping a low profile than anything else. I did engage in political activities that might have been considered illegal by some people. On the rare occasions when I was involved in violent confrontations, my actions never went beyond the need for self-defense.

From the late fifties through the seventies I was involved in every major demonstration in the cities where I lived. Fortunately, my experience with Pete's incarceration had left me with such an aversion to being locked up that I always managed to place myself just outside the zone where arrests were being made.

The Bay Area

By the early sixties I had given up on the idea of ever returning to New York. Surviving in Los Angeles was difficult enough; I couldn't imagine how it could be accomplished in New York. But I missed the energy of a real city. Los Angeles was an endless series of housing developments and malls strung together; some neighborhoods were more affluent than others but no part of it, even the so-called downtown, was really urban. I missed the sense of possibility that a city offered.

Susie was ready for a move as well. We talked it over and decided to relocate up North in the San Francisco Bay Area. Interestingly, many of our close friends had come to the same conclusion. Given that we were all involved in the movement, it wasn't surprising that we found San Francisco appealing. The urban environment, the physical beauty, and the celebrated tolerance for the unconventional, made the Bay Area a very attractive alternative to life in Southern California.

We rented an apartment in Berkeley. Susie attended classes at the University of California. She became active in the Free Speech Movement, spent a night sleeping-in at Sproul Hall, and just barely missed being arrested. After graduating in Anthropology she got a teaching credential and took a job in an elementary school. She became a creative and much sought after teacher.

Before moving up north, I had transferred from LACC, a junior college, to LA State College, a four-year institution. My ability to function in an academic environment had slowly improved so that by the time we got to the Bay Area I was able to attend San Francisco State University and eventually graduate with good grades in Sociology.

While we were in school we survived on part-time jobs, student aid, and an occasional check from Susie's parents. Like most of our friends, we changed residence every few months. It seemed as though every weekend someone needed help moving. The housing market was flexible enough to allow this settling in to occur regularly, and gradually the interval between our moves lengthened.

Berkeley was one of the first cities in the country to begin a serious effort to integrate the public schools. Middle and upper-middle class white families had settled in the hills. The less desirable flatland areas housed a mix of transient young whites and stable black families. The Berkeley integration plan called for the youngest students to be bussed to schools located in the hills. Conversely, the 4-6 students were bussed down from the hills to schools in the flatlands. This plan, though morally questionable, had the effect of mitigating some of the considerable white flight to private schools that had been set in motion by the integration efforts.

Like the tolerant ambiance of Hyde Park in Chicago, or the Village in New York, the liberal racial atmosphere in Berkeley attracted many interracial families. I discussed this situation with my mother and she agreed that the boys, now in their teens, would be far better off living in Berkeley. When Big Pete left for a visit to the Soviet Union, my mother moved up to Berkeley with Little Pete and Fred.

One night, not long after they moved, the phone rang. My mother was on the line and she was hysterical. Though she was shouting, her voice was barely audible because the sound came in waves that crested and then receded. I knew she was calling from Moscow. She had gone there to visit Pete, who by then was receiving acute medical care for tuberculosis and a heart condition.

Though I knew he would get better care there, when Pete left I suspected his real motive was to get a look at the *Promised Land* before it was too late. Between gasps and screams my mother confirmed that he was dead. She demanded that I come there immediately to attend a funeral and bring his remains back to America. She told me the Party would handle all the arrangements. When she said that, I knew arguing with her would be pointless. Once she had set the Party wheels in motion, my only choices were to go along with the program or never speak to her again.

Little Pete and Fred were staying with us. When I got off the phone I broke the news to them. They were a little older than I had been when my mother told me she wanted to marry Pete (old enough to understand in a general way what was happening but completely in the dark as to the consequences).

Susie said she would take care of the boys and

I packed a bag. I was in shock—not so much at Pete's death, I was expecting that—what had me completely disoriented was the abrupt interruption of my daily life. I had jumped out of bed in the middle of the night, and had begun packing for a trip half way around the world almost immediately after I had hung up the phone. By the time I caught my breath I was in the Russian version of a limo proceeding to the cremation ceremony.

There were a few Russians in attendance at the mausoleum. I assumed they were highly ranked Party members there to express their condolences. The Americans present, in addition to my mother and myself, included a few Communists or fellow travelers, who happened to be in Moscow at the time. Pete's life and accomplishments were recounted briefly; telegrams were read; the Russians issued their tributes to Pete, and then the body was rolled into the cremation oven. Pete's ashes were delivered to me at our hotel in an urn.

We left soon after that for New York. On the flight back my mother sat next to me. We hit a serious storm in the middle of the Atlantic, and the plane bumped and lurched around for what seemed like several hours. A couple of times gravity took control of the plane. During these stomach-wrenching altitude drops, I kept the urn securely locked between my legs. When we reached New York, I swore I would never fly again. I didn't hold to that resolution, but it was several decades before I could fly without experiencing major anxiety.

I turned the urn with Pete's ashes over to

someone from the Party in New York and continued home to California. The urn was transported to Chicago where it was interred along with the remains of the Haymarket martyrs and other American radicals.

IDENTITY

Considering identity

By the time I hit graduate school in the late sixties, the liberal ideology at the root of much of sociological theory had come under blistering attack. The middle class had crashed the gentlemen's club of postgraduate education, and many of these newly arrived students were primed to believe that elites were orchestrating the show. Michael Harrington, C. Wright Mills, and others, were winning over scores of students to a more radical perspective. I was still stating the obvious and risking being seen as having a coarse point of view, but I was no longer much of an outlier.

My views hadn't changed much; I still saw the world pretty much as I always had: the deck was obviously stacked. But my interest had shifted. I now wanted to understand how a person arrived at an identity. It had finally dawned on me that this was an empirical question. The pragmatists, John Dewey, George H. Mead, and others, had written about this problem and I started reading them. It wasn't just intellectual curiosity that propelled me; in my academic meanderings, I had come across a remarkable group of sociologists in San Francisco who were engaging in participant observation. These people became my colleagues and friends.

I had been hired on a project that was studying the *summer of love*. No one really knew what was going to happen in the Haight-Ashbury during the summer of 1967. But the fact that large numbers of young people had travelled there seemed to be the kind of thing sociologists should be paying attention to. A grant proposal was written, and when it was funded I was hired.

It wasn't the first time in history that an event like this had occurred. Mass migrations and ecstatic missions have been reported in ancient times, and they persist in the present era. They are usually motivated by religious pursuits of one sort or another. Granted: going to a party is not the same as going to church, nevertheless, for many young people who came to the Haight that summer, the journey was as much a quest as El Camino de Compostela or the Hajj.

The proximate cause of the exodus was a piece of performance art. Some members of the SF Mime troupe, and an assortment of anarchists who called themselves diggers, held a press conference on the steps of City Hall in San Francisco. The ostensible purpose was to urge the city authorities to prepare for the large influx of young people who were expected to come to the city that summer. The speakers at the press conference alleged that the city fathers were not preparing for the migration that was about to take place. At the time, no one in their right mind could have known that a hundred thousand people would actually show up. The press conference was a ruse foisted on the reporters who attended. Hungry for a story, these journalists saw to it that the word went out.

To its credit, the greater Bay Area community did its best to accommodate these kids when they did start to show up in large numbers. Free meals, a free clinic, free clothing stores and crash pads all materialized, seemingly out of nowhere. My rational side knew that the community that was emerging in the Haight was unsustainable, but my emotions were with it all the way. I suppose this was true of most of the people who were involved. We all knew we were sustaining a fantasy, yet our daily lives were affirming the reality of the fantasy.

The way the community functioned was easy to observe. The farmers who came to the San Francisco Produce Market usually had unsold food left over, and they were happy to donate it rather than see it rot. All it took to feed large numbers of people were a few volunteers who picked up the leftover food, prepared it, and then distributed it. The provision of other surplus goods and services followed a similar pattern.

Euphoria was the order of the day, and we were all swept away. The professor who was reading my field notes published an article entitled: *Why we may all be hippies someday.* The diggers, a loose confederation of people with anarchist sympathies who managed the resources, became minor cultural heroes. Before any of us saw it coming, however, the joy was sapped out of the community by a drug called *speed.*

If I hadn't accepted it earlier, I became certain things had changed for the worse the day I talked with two men who I knew were drug dealers. They starting discussing a guy I didn't know, and they came to the conclusion that something needed to be done to keep him from ripping people off. The conversation ended with one of them saying, "I'll get my gun."

I hadn't kept the fact that I was doing research a secret. I had learned pretty quickly that most people didn't care, as long as I went about doing pretty much the same things they were doing. But the lack of caution these guys exhibited surprised me; they had no way of knowing that I wasn't a cop. When the one who remained offered me a drink, I was quick to accept. It didn't take me long to realize that my attempt to put him at ease was a mistake; I had been drugged.

Luckily, I was able to stagger over to a friend's apartment before I passed out. I never saw either of these dealers again, and I never learned whether their threat had been carried out. By the time I was fully recovered, I had made up my mind that I knew more than I wanted to know about the changes taking place in the Haight-Ashbury.

The apartment where I recovered belonged to Patrick Biernacki. Patrick and I had met in graduate school at SF State, and we became close friends after we both enrolled in the PhD program at UCSF. Patrick had grown up in Chicago. His father was an alcoholic, and his mother washed floors to support the family. He was charismatic and fearless. He had been a dangerous criminal as a teenager, but he abandoned that hopeless trajectory by moving to California.

A life-long substance abuser, Patrick became a well-known addiction researcher who pioneered important sampling techniques. When the AIDS crisis hit he was instrumental in coming up with a plan that taught addicts to disinfect their works with bleach. There is no doubt that he helped save many lives.

Patrick had many endearing qualities that drew people to him. His most appealing trait, in my view at least, was his absolute and forceful resistance to the culture of academia. He was capable of delivering a paper at one of the annual sociological meetings that began, "Youse guys."

Over the years Patrick went from one project to the next, doing extraordinary work in each, without accumulating a reputation that would make his life easier. Many of his colleagues attributed his lack of success to his heavy use of drugs and alcohol. I never knew him to be unreliable; he was intractable, sometimes belligerent, but he always followed through on the work he was expected to do.

Patrick was an extreme narcissist who would not adopt the views of those of us, including his doctors, who tried to get him to stop killing himself. We simply could not get through to him. The fact that he was loved and respected by many of us for his resistance to upper middle class culture may have contributed to the difficulty he had in changing his behavior. But I believe he never really wanted to change. His death, at a relatively early age, was the direct result of his drug and alcohol abuse.

The well known psycho-social explanations for Patrick's intransigence, even in combination, didn't feel right to me. How he had become the person I knew was a complete mystery to me, though I knew him as well as anyone could know a close friend. And if I was unable to understand how Patrick defined his life, how could I do so for the young people I was studying?

I concluded that one can't know, in some scientifically verifiable way, how people go about constructing an identity. What I did know about these young people was that they were very vague about who they were. I don't think this was just a matter of their not being able to report clearly; I think they just weren't sure. They may have spoken, dressed, and acted, in similar ways but when push came to shove, I believe they were all searching for an identity.

Western culture doesn't provide a well-defined ceremony signaling the transition to adulthood. There is a long period, or *moratorium*, when one's role is uncertain. This makes it difficult to see oneself clearly. The summer of love occurred just as the baby-boom generation was passing through late adolescence. If living was easy, and the future not clearly perceived, there didn't appear to be any reason to fear what might happen next and that made planning unnecessary. Living in—and for—the moment was the order of the day. Fog wasn't just a physical manifestation of the Haight-Ashbury landscape; it was the psychological state of many of the inhabitants; it characterized the way people went about construing and constructing their daily lives.

This way of living may have been more pronounced among the so-called hippies, but vagueness about identity, about who we are, isn't extraordinary. We are never just one thing. Straight-jacketing the self in one all-consuming identity freezes a life.

Perhaps late in life, when reflecting on an abundance of living, a person might be inclined to sum up who he is. If anything, that exercise, happening as it does in the face of death, would be the exception. Most of the time, most of us are too busy dealing with the fastballs and curves coming at us for that kind of self-reflection.

I know someone who, having seen the same psychoanalyst for more than fifty years, feels that there is still much more work to be done. I suppose I'm describing something that could be called psychosocial indeterminacy. This idea—that we can't know in some scientifically verifiable way exactly how each human being creates meaning—is something I began to really appreciate during my first attempt to do participant observation. This realization led me to begin doubting the entire sociological enterprise.

Losing the front

Susie and I moved back to Berkeley from San Francisco. She had a job teaching in a public elementary school there, and I was working as a longshoreman. The docks were booming thanks to the war in Vietnam. Most of the members of the International Longshoreman's and Warehouseman's Union were leftists and many of them couldn't or wouldn't work the army bases. But in those pre-container days, there was more than enough non-military work to keep everyone busy.

Each morning I would head for the shape-up at the union hall in San Francisco. Once all the union members had accepted jobs, the social security men (non-members, like me, who could present a social security card) would be hired. The best jobs went to the union men with the most seniority, and by the time the shape-up got around to us, only the most undesirable jobs were left. We were happy to take them because the pay was good.

Many of these jobs were physically taxing; they involved moving difficult cargo (maggot-infested, slippery animal hides, or heavy sacks of coffee beans). We usually labored below deck, moving the load by hand to and from pallets that were raised and lowered by the ship's crane into the hold. The work was very dangerous.

Though we were usually exhausted after a few

hours the camaraderie among the workers made the job tolerable. During the breaks, and at lunch times, the men would tell stories about legendary longshoremen who were experts at cargo shrinkage. A lot of the talk was hot air but the underlying themes (stealing is just getting even) usually underscored important moral lessons. I had little doubt that a good deal of theft was taking place. On the ships I worked there was very little serious security; then again who would want to take home a maggot-infested hide?

Most of the A men (the longshoremen with the most seniority) had a long-term partner. The men were usually hired in gangs to work a specific section of a ship. All the personal relationships flowed from this procedure. The partner arrangement allowed for flexibility in hiring and scheduling, and it assured stability in the way the work would be handled. I had never come across friendships like these. These partners knew one another as well as anyone could know another person. They relied on one another for their livelihood and safety; their very lives depended on the health of their relationships.

Around this time cocaine was becoming available in large quantities. Some of it was coming in on ships. For a few longshoremen with the right connections, and a desire to live even more dangerously, the job could be quite lucrative. The only problem was the money brought with it the threat of violence. It seemed to me, once again, that drugs were symptomatic of something else: an un-easiness many of these longshoremen were experiencing.

The guys who took the longer view, and there was a surprising number of them, knew that life on the docks was about to change drastically. The shipping companies were investing in equipment that would change the way cargo was loaded. Giant container ships were being built that could take on cargo that would be handled solely by huge dockside cranes. These containers would be filled and emptied at sites far removed from coastal cities.

Though the union responded to this challenge by protecting its members (negotiating contracts that trained men in the new equipment and provided decent pensions for those who retired) the lively fraternity created by the gangs working in the holds inexorably began disappearing. The once-thriving social life of longshoremen became, seemingly overnight, the alienating labor of people working in isolation: operating cranes and driving container forklifts.

What was about to be lost was not measurable in financial terms. A life that was given meaning by the necessity of caring for and relying on one's partners was disappearing. The new way of working may have been monetarily rewarding, but it had very little to recommend it on the social side. Being able to identify oneself, in the midst of similar others, as a person who is relied upon and valued—a situation that dock workers had been nurturing through lore and practice for many generations—was about to disappear forever.

All my adult life I have done my best to avoid social occasions where strangers mill around and encounter one another. No doubt some of my reluctance has to do with my natural instinct for invisibility. But there is more to it than that. Sooner or later the conversation naturally gravitates to the question, "So, what do you do?"

I remember discussing this with Allen Sillitoe the author of *The Loneliness of a Long Distance Runner*. Sillitoe told me he had solved the problem by saying he is a surveyor. He had discovered that this answer usually succeeded in changing the subject.

It isn't just that the question gives you important information about what the person does for a living. It may (and usually does) suffice to tell the asker who the person is. This is particularly useful for knowing what tone to take in the conversation. But it freezes the interaction and distorts perceptions of the responder's other identities.

Like most young adults, during this time in my life, work couldn't define who I was. I drove a cab; I was a teaching assistant; I worked on the docks; everything I was paid to do was, from my point of view, a temporary job. The identity conferred by these jobs entailed a very distorted image of me. I objected to locating myself in this way because I was aware that the game that was being played (if interactions between people can be viewed as a game) included a deck that was stacked against people like me. My jobs were at the bottom of the social totem pole. The fact that I preferred to be an isolate rather than find myself in situations in which I was condescended to was probably a very healthy response.

A career without an identity

For a few years I worked as an adjunct instructor at SF State and Cal State Hayward. The economy was in recession and tenure track jobs were few and far between. Thanks in part to white-flight, Sonoma County was the fastest growing area in the country and the college there (Sonoma State) was in the midst of a hiring binge. In 1974 I managed to snag one of their tenure-track jobs. A new, more secure, world was opening before me. Later that year our son Dov was born.

Most of the other new hires had been graduate students during the sixties. This set up a town and gown disconnect that rivaled those in the middle ages. Luckily, there was a small cohort of faculty who, like me, couldn't force themselves to live in Sonoma County. I commuted with these Berkeley people, and over time formed close friendships with several of them. The fact that all of my new friends were respected members of the faculty encouraged me to begin to view myself as someone who might actually belong in academic life. Since there were several tenured people in my department who had neither published nor acquired a PhD, I told myself I had already achieved far more than the Department's minimal standard.

I had abandoned the idea that sociology represented a viable way of coming to terms with the human condition. It seemed it me that there were other ways of understanding, particularly in the arts, that came closer to capturing the meaning of experience. Continuing to teach a discipline that no longer fired your imagination was probably not a good idea. I told myself that I would make the most of my job; I would use it as an opportunity to give my students the critical skills they would need to make their lives meaningful. Most importantly, I would try to model intellectual curiosity. That meant getting off the pedestal—asking questions I didn't have an answer for—and giving my students room to form their own perspectives.

Given enough time, and the vagaries of an academic career, I probably could have constructed a viable identity had it not been for the fact that the University got a new President whose avowed goal was to turn the institution into "the Harvard of the West."

The University Trustees bought this whopper hook, line, and sinker. The faculty reaction was mixed. Many of the new President's supporters were status climbers and sycophants. The most self-assured members of the faculty saw it, rightly in my opinion, as an attempt to denigrate their achievements in order to grab power.

After teaching for the usual probationary period, I applied for tenure. My application was reviewed by the requisite committees and forwarded to the President who then met with me. He kept me waiting quite a long time. When I was finally ushered into his office he came straight to the point: asking me why I thought he should grant me tenure. I told him (what he already knew but didn't want to hear) that the reason he should grant me tenure was that each of the faculty committees had recommended it. Our meeting ended shortly thereafter.

I didn't have a good feeling about the meeting, but I told myself that he wouldn't have the nerve to fly in the face of the faculty recommendations. I was wrong; later that summer I received a letter from him saying that he was denying tenure for "programmatic" reasons. Apparently he had decided, probably on the basis of my low profile, that he could make an example of me without taking too much flak. I already had too much invested to allow that to happen.

The Fall Convocation was the only meeting during the year that involved the entire faculty. When the President addressed the faculty that Fall, announcing that the anticipated budget cuts wouldn't require lay-offs of permanent faculty, I shouted, "That's a lie." There was a stunned silence. As far as I knew no one had ever done anything remotely like that before. I probably should have stood up and argued with him at that point but I didn't have the courage. No doubt many in the audience felt my outburst was a cowardly thing.

It didn't take long for the gossip network to establish who had done the shouting. By countermanding the tenure recommendations of three faculty committees the President was challenging the structure of governance of the University. My actions managed to make the whole thing personal, and from then on the President had it in for me. But my outburst had an upside: all of my colleagues were now aware of my situation and some of them were willing to support me. The budget crisis had shaken everyone. Though most faculty members are usually complacent about campus politics everyone was now wide-awake, and each person had a very real stake in what the President was attempting. Everyone understood that he wasn't just making a quirky decision in my case; he was sending a message to the entire faculty.

Basically my strategy was to conduct a guerilla war. A group of advisors came forward, and they helped me fight my way through the elaborate grievance process. As the last person hired in my department, I was the one without any courses when our budget was finalized. To remain viable economically, and to retain a profile on campus while I fought, I had to cobble together courses in other departments. Each semester I would start in a new department, teach a course or two, and then the budget of that department would be cut. In all, I ended up teaching in five different departments during this period, each of the new courses required a different preparation and an adjustment in the identity I projected: I became an instructor in psychology, philosophy, film criticism, and education.

If I hadn't already known what it was like to be a pariah, and how to deal with it, I probably wouldn't have survived the experience. Before I arrived at Sonoma another faculty member who had been denied tenure had committed suicide. Part of me felt

I deserved what had happened. I had been cutting it pretty thin in the past, and the new pressures were making it impossible for me to do an exemplary job. On the other hand, Sonoma was not the Harvard of the West. At my flakiest, I was more productive than some of my tenured colleagues. I was pretty sure my political attitudes had a lot to do with my situation. That thought was reassuring but I knew that most of my supporters believed there was too much smoke for the fire to be completely absent. This awareness kept me awake the better part of many nights.

During this time the University was in constant turmoil; while I was fighting the President's decision, most of the Deans, Vice Presidents, and many of the lower administrators resigned. With the support of my colleagues I was able to slog my way through the grievance process. In the end, all the grievance committees agreed that I should be granted tenure. The President refused to accept the grievance committees' recommendations. We went to binding arbitration. The arbitrator agreed with my position. The President refused to accept the arbitrator's decision. Then the Chancellor's office, fearing a major lawsuit, intervened and ordered him to grant me tenure.

By the time I was awarded tenure, the institutional crisis had reached its peak. I was elected to serve on the Executive Committee of the Academic Senate, and we censured the President. After that the Chancellor removed him. He was given an office at San Francisco State with no responsibilities. Later, he was hired as President of Adelphi College in New

York. He precipitated a crisis there; he was investigated for misappropriating resources and he was dismissed from that position as well.

I came away from this struggle with a bittersweet feeling about myself as an academic. I had gained a sinecure, one that would support me for the rest of my life. Though I wasn't a scholar I knew there was other important work to be done in my University. I started working regularly with graduate students who were preparing for or enhancing their teaching careers. I respected the choices these people had made and I endeavored to help them achieve their goals. Most importantly I tried to help them understand the really hard to reach students. I felt that my own experience, though I very rarely shared it directly, was of value in helping them work with these students.

I remained at Sonoma for thirty years and then I retired with emeritus status. I was never comfortable being Professor Rizzo; it was an identity I had earned the hard way, but it was not an identity that came close to capturing who I was.

Goodbye to the Mayor

My uncle Georgie called. As soon as I heard his voice, I knew it was bad news. A couple of months earlier my father had called from a hospital to tell me he was having trouble breathing. He was worried because the doctors couldn't figure out what was wrong with him. He asked me to come to New York. It was the first time he had ever said he needed me. My father had been missing so much of my life my first impulse had been to cop out on him. But I knew he cared about me; he was just too passive a person to push his way into my life. So I got on a plane and flew to New York. When I visited him in the hospital we hadn't had much to talk about. That didn't matter; he let me know he was going to die, not in words, by the look in his eyes. When we said goodbye I knew it was for the last time.

"Your father died this morning."

I told Georgie I wanted to come for the funeral. Without my having to ask, he said he would wire the money for the plane ticket. The bars, and the OTB, took all of the money my old man had, so there was no chance he was leaving a pile of money for a big send-off. Though Georgie and I never spoke about money, I figured there was probably just enough for the burial and the plane ticket.

A limo picked me up at the airport and took me straight to the cemetery. There were a few of my father's friends, my uncles, and cousins at the funeral chapel. Georgie spoke and said that his brother was one of the gentlest men he knew and that he had never done anything to hurt another human being. What he was saying was true. Then he asked if anyone had anything to say. No one did.

Then Georgie went over to the foot of the casket, where there was a rolled up flag, and he handed the flag to me. I tucked it under my arm. Then I followed Georgie back to the casket. Everyone got up and formed a line behind us. When I got close to the casket I was drawn to my father and something made me bend down and kiss his cheek. It was as if I was a child again saying goodbye on Sunday afternoon.

I wasn't expecting his skin to be cold. I backed away. My lips were tingling. I felt as though some virus was coursing through my body. Uncle Georgie nodded that I was supposed to stand next to him. Each person in the crowd strolled past the casket and shook hands with me. I didn't make eye contact with any of my father's friends; I didn't want to make believe that these strangers meant a whole lot to me.

A bunch of us carried it out to the hearse. We all got into cars and drove over to the gravesite. Grandpa Rizzo had been looking to the future when he bought the family plot. There was just enough room for him, his wife, and their children to be buried here. Now, with the hole they dug for my father, there was only room for my uncles. That was fine with me; I didn't have any reason to be stacked up next to them.

I said goodbye to my cousin Theresa and Uncle Patsy. Then Georgie walked me back to my limo. I had been wondering whether Aunt Mary would show up. She and my mother hadn't said a word to each other since Grandma's funeral. When I asked Georgie about her, he said he had heard she was married and had moved up to Newburgh. I knew her husband's last name and I got their number from information when I got to the airport.

The woman who answered sounded just like Mary, but she denied being my aunt. I pleaded with her but she was adamant so I hung up. It must have been hard for her to deny who she was because I was certain that, when I was a kid, she had loved me.

The trip back to California was another plane ride from hell; we bounced around the sky like a pinball. Strangely, though I was sure I was going to die, I didn't scream or get out of my seat. That would have been too embarrassing. It isn't exactly comforting to think that I was capable of going to my death without making some kind of complaint. I suppose that's because I truly am my father's son.

Letting go

Susie attended a women's group for a while. I avoided this kind of *support* like the plague having witnessed Communist Party meetings as a kid. The idea of getting together with people simply because they happened to be my gender appealed to me about as much as attending a whites only prayer-breakfast.

But we both needed help. There were issues in our marriage that needed to be addressed. We saw several therapists. Eventually I made it through a few group therapy sessions and a marathon. Most of the couples we encountered in therapy were dealing with sexual fidelity in one form or another. I don't think I'd ever actively espoused monogamy. I didn't require it, nor did I practice it. We had never agreed that we would have affairs, but we both had them, and we were aware that the other person was having them. I ignored the issue; it seemed to me to be the best way to minimize the inevitable jealousies.

Our dissatisfaction with one another wasn't just sexual; other aspects of the relationship were also problematic. I felt that Susie was too dependent on me, and I believe Susie felt I was unreliable and distant. Though we weren't happy in the marriage, it took us years to decide to divorce. I think we were both aware that we would be losing a person with many positive qualities. Over the years we gradually drifted apart and eventually I had had enough and so had Susie.

Though we had some disagreement over the property settlement, we found a solution both of us could live with. The real matter that concerned us was the custody arrangement. We both came to the conclusion that joint custody was the best solution for Dov, who was then five years old. Joint physical custody had only recently become a legal possibility in California and we agreed to try a 50/50 split.

Since Susie and I were in accord we decided to save money and not involve any lawyers in the process (yet another California legal innovation). On the appointed day we both showed up in court and presented materials that a legal counselor had helped us prepare.

The judge examined our agreement and then said he was awarding full custody to Susie. I was furious, and I started shouting incoherently. The judge warned me that if I didn't control my outburst he would have me arrested. I told him that I didn't understand how he could do what he was planning to do. His response was that we obviously didn't understand what we were doing.

Luckily, I realized that he was giving me an opening. I acknowledged that he was right, that I didn't understand the process, and that I needed the advice of an attorney. I pleaded with him to reschedule the hearing so that I could have an opportunity to hire counsel. He turned to Susie and told her that he was prepared to award her custody right then and there—or if she preferred he would allow us both to hire legal representation and return at another time.

To my relief Susie told him she preferred the latter course. I will always remember, and be thankful for, her wisdom at that moment. We both hired attorneys and we came back to a different courtroom presided over by a different judge. When we presented what was essentially the original agreement the judge had no objection, and it was approved.

The frailty of my father's grip on me may have been responsible for my strong need to hold on to Dov. Though I really can't say what brought it about, I am certain that I was determined to make a go of joint custody. During our separation and after the divorce I believe I succeeded in being a good father. I tried to provide a reasonably healthy environment for my son and to satisfy his educational and emotional needs. For the first time in my life, I was committed to an identity I could admire.

Upper Level

My house on Grant Street was a short walk up the hill to Mr. Peet's. Alfred Peet sold these dark roasts that appealed to the addicted. I started buying coffee there around the time a couple of guys who knew Mr. Peet also started buying his roasts for their new business in Seattle, a store called Starbucks. I liked going up to Peet's because it was one of several interesting gourmet type businesses that gave North Berkeley a definite European small town feel.

The thing about Peet's was that it didn't have a view. It was located on the ground floor of an old Victorian that was part of group of buildings surrounding an inner courtyard. The complex was called Walnut Square. There was a restaurant in the courtyard, *The Egg Shop and Apple Press*, with a deck upstairs that was known as the *Upper Level*. From the *Upper Level* you had a view of the bay and the Golden Gate. When the weather was nice, it was a great place to sit, read, talk, and drink coffee. The place appealed to Berkeley types: graduate students, would-be artists, itinerant academics, and an occasional Nobel Prize winner. Most of the regulars qualified as dyed-in-the-wool bohemians.

I had several male friends who frequented the place, guys with advanced degrees who were cobbling together an existence selling Derrida and Lacan to the masses. Sometimes the bullshit at the Upper Level rose to extraordinary levels, and when it did the sparks would fly. But the conversations didn't always involve verbal pyrotechnics; most of the time we talked about the mundane topics of daily life. This was as it should be; a coffee house full of regulars is really just one big surrogate family.

Not long after I started going there I noticed a young woman who came there often. She had a huge natural that surrounded her head like a Renaissance halo. The fact that it was a deeply red made her very hard to miss. Also hard to miss was her taste in reading material; it was about as highbrow as you could get. I wanted to meet her but she never engaged in conversation with any of the regulars; she was always alone, and she seemed to like it that way. Since I wasn't about to walk up to a good-looking woman with some break-the-ice type line, I had no way of getting to know her. So we sat there: neither of us emitting the slightest gesture—no smile of recognition, no eye contact—that might provide an opening that could lead to more.

We read our way through book after book, journal after journal, day after day, week after week, and month after month. Finally, about six months after I had first spied her, I could take it no longer, and I did what was very difficult for me: I broke the ice by asking about some article she was reading in the *New York Review*. Her response was a little standoffish but polite enough for me to pursue the conversation and gradually we both loosened up. I learned that her name was Wendy Lesser. After a few minutes she told me she had to attend a seminar on campus and she got up to leave. With my heart pounding, I asked if she wanted company on the walk over to campus (I was actually planning to leave in an entirely different direction). She agreed to let me tag along, and we set off. By the time we got to the campus I knew that we were going to hit it off. Very soon after that we became lovers.

She was the most brilliant person I had ever met. She didn't display it in obvious ways; it just popped out at you in the middle of a normal conversation. She was about to get a PhD in English at Berkeley after having been at Harvard and Cambridge. She had just started a small consulting business with her friend Katharine Ogden, also a graduate student in English. They could think and write clearly, and it seems these skills were in short supply at the social service groups who funded their reports.

We saw one another frequently after that first day. We usually talked about the subjects that interested us most: politics and art. I was proud of my independent perspective. I rarely wavered from a strong point of view on an issue that mattered. I was completely dazzled by Wendy; her opinions seemed even more deeply felt than mine. She rarely expressed uncertainty. Occasionally, she might shift the footing of an argument as it progressed, but she was always first out of starting gate and invariably on the money. More often than not when we disagreed about an actual fact, I would discover that she had been right.

We were good for one another. Her gregarious nature drew people to us. Her friends became my friends. When I was with her I could participate comfortably without having to call a lot of attention to myself. I think I was useful for her, socially, as well. She was attached to a desirable male who didn't have a strong need to dominate.

Wendy did a good job of steering clear of confrontations with Dov. She didn't try to control him or demand affection. At first I resented the fact that she kept her distance. Then I saw that this was the best approach, particularly in light of the difficulties Dov was having with Susie's new husband. Given that chaos is Wendy's number one adversary— she never passes up an opportunity to organize—this was a remarkable accomplishment.

We had been living together five or six years. I was in my mid-forties, and Wendy was twelve years younger. Putting off having a child wasn't a good idea so we stopped using birth control. Our son Nick was conceived not long after that. We married at San Francisco City Hall; our wedding day coincided with the weekend that the Forty-Niners were playing in the Superbowl down at Stanford. Most of the people in the line with us had scheduled their weddings to coincide with the game. The hallway outside the judge's chambers resembled the line outside the Fillmore Auditorium on a Saturday night. It was one big, happy, San Francisco party.

By the time Nick was born, Wendy was already well on her way to a career as a writer. Single-handedly she founded, published, and edited, *The*

Threepenny Review, now one of the oldest independently run arts quarterlies in America. She has authored a number of books on a variety of subjects in the arts and she has been honored with many awards and speaking invitations.

I think my desire for invisibility is one of the reasons our relationship works. I can barely imagine the pain for both of us that would have ensued had I tried to compete with Wendy for attention as a writer. I know I'm not the only invisible writer out there. In fact, I believe the visible writers—the people who announce their calling—are merely the tip of a huge iceberg. Laboring beneath the surface, as I have for many years, has taught me to respect what I do and to try to do it well. This is certainly not a unique realization, far from it, but it has given meaning to my life.

Rose alone

My mother could not have successfully raised two children of mixed race and me in those difficult times if her character had been wishy-washy. She was one of the strongest people I have ever known. When an idea became fixed in her consciousness there was very little that could be done to dislodge it.

I don't think Rose ever formally left the Communist Party. By the late fifties it was obvious to anyone who was paying attention that something was terribly wrong in Russia. After Pete died, my mother gradually loosened her ties with the organization. She blamed the Stalinists for the failures. I think she meant by this the ideological dogmatists, and the bureaucrats who followed them: people who were blind to reality and unable to make realistic, humane choices. Miraculously, her dissatisfaction with the Party hadn't resulted in cynicism; she remained steadfast in her belief that ultimately the underclass would be liberated, though it was probably clear to her that this would never come about in her lifetime.

Rose hadn't changed very much over the years, but the times certainly had. Almost without any of us seeming to notice it had become possible to associate with someone of another race in a public place and not have to be constantly on guard. With those pressures, and the burden of being the wife of a prominent Communist, no longer weighing on her

Rose could afford to pay attention to the needs of others. Somehow, perhaps through my brothers, she acquired a circle of young friends. She helped as many these young progressive kids as she could, sharing her meager resources with them and seeing to it that they landed on their feet. The only characteristic she had in common with these kids was the fact that they were rebelling. She identified with that and that was what made her an effective mentor.

Rose had asked me to come over. I knew something was up and I didn't have to wait long to find out. She opened the door, told me to sit down, and as her eyes filled with tears she said, "My doctor says I have lung cancer."

I asked if she was sure. She told me she had already been given a second opinion that confirmed the original diagnosis. Then, just as I might have expected, she bravely went on to talk matter-of-factly about the arrangements she was making for the disposition of her property. I let her go on like this, trying my best not to allow my emotions to intrude on the practical tone she had adopted. We agreed on what I was supposed to do for her and then I said goodbye. The only sign that anything extraordinary had occurred was the length of the hug she gave me at her door.

Word of my mother's death came during the Christmas holiday. I took out an ad in the Communist newspaper to announce her death, and I told a few of her friends about a memorial service that my brothers had organized. I attended the service but didn't participate. As usual, I preferred to remain as invisible as possible. I suppose these memorials provide a sense of closure for people. I prefer to mourn silently and in isolation.

The service was held in a black church in Oakland. When the room began to fill up with people of different races I wasn't surprised. The real eye opener was the number of young people who showed up to pay their respects. One after another they got up and told stories of how my mother had helped them get their lives together. Hearing all these kids talk about her, and remembering how unselfish she could be, I was overwhelmed with sorrow at her death. For all her craziness, she had succeeded in living a life that was useful to others.

In 1989, about a year after her death, I came across the following story in the *New York Times*:

A 16 year-old black youth was shot to death Wednesday night in an attack by 10 to 30 white teen-agers in the Bensonhurst section of Brooklyn. The whites, the authorities said, were lying in wait for black or Hispanic youths who they thought were dating a white neighborhood girl. But the victim was not involved with the girls, the police said, and had come to the predominantly white neighborhood with three black friends to look at a used car.

I thought of my friend Abe who lived across the street from us when I was a child. His religion, if he still practiced it, might have allowed him to retain some humanity in the face of such narrow-mindedness. If Abe had been around when they were trying to kill that young man, perhaps he would have tried to stop it. But I have my doubts.

I know one thing: Rose's decision to marry Pete provided me with a unique vantage point from which to watch the unfolding of American history. Luckily my desire for invisibility—probably a necessary survival mechanism given the situation—didn't make the suffering of others invisible to me. Not seeing the misery around me would have made it much easier to disappear. Now, when I am told about certain characteristics that adhere to certain kinds of people, my hair stands up on the back of my neck but I no longer feel I have to hide. I find a way to communicate how limited such views are. I have Rose and Pete to thank for providing me with that ability.

Post Script

Frail, on the worn sand,
a wind swept bubble hides: bursts.
Spring tide here again.

I retired from teaching at Sonoma State University in 2002. Nick was off to college and Wendy's career was transportable: we were free to leave Berkeley for extended periods. We leased a tiny apartment in the Village and began a bicoastal life. In that year I lost significant aspects of my identity. I was a father whose kids were grown, a person without a vocation, and now I no longer had one place I could call home. Perhaps that is why I considered learning the Italian language.

I decided to enroll in an Italian Class at the Borough of Manhattan Community College. The application required that I provide transcripts from every college I had attended. I knew that it would be very difficult to locate all these documents, so I met with an admissions officer and presented the letter that appointed me to emeritus status at Sonoma. That did the trick and I was admitted.

My first day of class turned out to be a wonderful learning experience. None of the other students was even close to half my age. There was only one other person in the class who was not Asian, Hispanic, or black: he turned out to be a recent Russian émigré. Strangely, or perhaps not, I felt completely at home in this environment. Everyone seemed to accept me; no special attention, deference, or hostility was directed at me. I was perfectly visible and invisible at the same time.

Dreading the test that was to come at the end of the first week I studied like mad. It turned out my score was just below that of the star in the class: a young Asian man. English was his second language and Italian his third. Though he had a full time job, and several children that he was helping raise, he always managed to score a little higher than me. Being competitive with this twenty-something, even though I knew he would probably come out on top, fueled my studies. After the semester was over I returned to Berkeley. I found a class there and later, as an advanced student, I found groups on both coasts to help me further my Italian language skills.

My interest in things Italian didn't begin with my language studies. Many years earlier I had written an article about doing oral histories with Italian Americans that was published in a journal called *Italian Americana*. My motivation to write the article came from some experiences I had while attending meetings of a group called the Italian American Historical Association.

I had heard about the group on the radio. Usually I jumped back and forth between a few favorite stations, but one day I happened to be moving through the dial slowly and a familiar aria, maybe from *Madame Butterfly*, made me stop. It wasn't that I was sure of the tune; what kept me from turning the dial was the way the music affected me emotionally. I first heard opera at my father's house during those Sunday dinners, and from then on whenever I heard the human voice in an Italian aria I would respond with this feeling of deep familiarity.

The memory—it was a feeling more than an actual memory—was so strong that I just sat there listening. When the music stopped a woman began speaking in Italian. I tried to make out what she was saying—and though I caught a word here and there—the thing that captured my attention was the soothing rhythm of her speech. It rolled out at me from the radio like little ripples on the surface of a lake. After a while the rhythm changed and I became aware that she had switched to English.

She was talking about a planned meeting of the Italian American Historical Association. She gave a phone number. There was a pencil next to the radio and I wrote it down. After that I thought about calling several times but couldn't bring myself to do it. Curiosity got the better of me and I finally broke down and called. The guy who answered was so aggressive that he got me to promise to come to their next meeting.

The meeting was held in the private dining room of a North Beach restaurant. After some milling around we all took seats around a large table. Not long after the meeting began I was asked what had made me want to attend. I wasn't up to telling them about the aria, and the time warp it put me in, so I took a gulp of air and said, "My grandparents were born in Italy, but I never learned much about being Italian. I was hoping I could learn a little more here."

It wasn't the whole truth; I couldn't tell these strangers that my education in becoming Italian American had been interrupted by having to move to Harlem. But the explanation wasn't a lie either. I was telling them enough of what they needed to hear for them to begin to see me for who I was. Bringing in the freak show—even though it might be truer to the facts—wasn't going to help them get to know me any better.

One of the participants said, "You know, Richie, most of us are in the same boat. That's why we're all here. It's the blind leading the blind."

I laughed, saying, "Well then I definitely qualify."

I knew my laugh was a little off, but I figured they were expecting me to be nervous, so, in a way, I was playing the tune they wanted to hear.

While I had been talking, the people on my side of the table had been twisting their necks, straining to make eye contact with me. They did this, I guess, because they wanted me to know they were interested in me. Now that I was finished speaking they had satisfied looks; clearly they were pleased with what I had said. Two of the older ladies were giving me especially warm looks, the kind of look reserved for a favorite nephew. The leader of the group was beaming brotherly love at me even though he was trying to keep things somewhat formal.

As the leader started to speak a grin appeared on his *business-as-usual* face. The grin gradually expanded from the edge of his lips up toward the center of his cheek until it was a full smile. "Then this will interest you, Riccardo, we need to talk about Columbus Day."

He rolled the last R in Riccardo. By saying my name in Italian like that he was trying to make me feel that I belonged. Only it didn't sound right. I wasn't *Riccardo*; Richie was a better name for me. It was plainer, and it didn't make me into something I wasn't. When I was younger, on a basketball court, or when I was just hanging out, white guys usually called me Rizzo. It was never with the Italian *Reetzo* pronunciation. Only a guy fresh off the boat would have used that. Often whites even mispronounced the Americanized version: guys seemed to get a kick out of saying Roozo or Rossio, and, later, there was Ratzo. As far as I could tell, non-Italians seemed to enjoy some little joke that went with saying my name incorrectly.

Instead of making me feel like a stranger—what you would think using someone's last name would do—it made people feel like they knew me, and the more comfortable they felt with me, the more they used it. It gave them a picture of who I was, and even though the picture had very little to do with who I was, I didn't try to change it. As long as they couldn't see who I really was, I felt in control.

Some black people called me Rizzo too, mostly in sports where it wasn't unusual to use someone's last name. But, after moving to Harlem, I was usually Richie with people who knew me. Being a Rizzo inside a black world didn't make the same kind of sense that it did in a white one. There was no way, when I was in Harlem, that I could be seen as the simple guy, locked into the small Italian-American world, that my name implied.

I knew that if I didn't correct the leader right then I was going to be Riccardo in this group forever. What could I do? If I made a big deal of it, I would end up souring the mood. After what I had said about why I had come there I couldn't reject a name that was so Italian sounding. But the truth was there was no way I was a Riccardo. In the end, I made up my mind to let it pass, and the leader went on with what he was saying.

His smile was gone and his voice began to reveal a deeper emotion. "Every day you hear people talking about the Mafia. That's what makes this Columbus Day celebration so important. If we don't show them there are other kinds of Italians they'll go on thinking we're all Mafosi."

They talked about the celebration for a while and then I excused myself, telling them I had to get home. I had a strong feeling of kinship with these people. This obviously didn't come from my knowing a lot about the specifics of their lives; my feeling was simply the result of the knowledge of our shared ancestry. The leader was right; our last names guaranteed that many people would immediately think Mafia when they met us. No other group of people could have understood exactly how I felt about that.

With the civil rights movement unraveling, I had attended these meetings in the hope of finding people I belonged with. We were alike in many ways but I couldn't worship my ancestry in the way these people did. What they were doing wasn't wrong; it was just that I had travelled too far to find it easy to identify with them. I would need to know a whole lot more about being Italian before I could even begin to think of myself as Italian American.

Italians were already the largest ethnic group in America by the time the discriminatory immigration legislation of the 1920's halted the great wave of emigration from Southern Europe. All of these immigrants, if they were to become U.S. citizens, had to formally renounce their Italian citizenship. My father, who was born in the U.S. before my grandfather renounced his Italian citizenship, was eligible for dual citizenship. As his son, I was eligible as well. In 2011, thanks to having located my grandfather's birth record—and more than ten years after I began accumulating the necessary documents—I acquired an Italian passport and became a citizen of two countries.

Occasionally, one of my friends would ask why I was studying Italian or applying for citizenship. I would explain that learning a language was good for my brain, or that it gave me something to do, or that by acquiring Italian citizenship I could pass on to my descendants the opportunity to be employed in the European common market. Sometimes I would semi-seriously joke about being able to leave the country if things went haywire.

None of these explanations really went to the heart of the matter. The truth was I was tired of hiding; I wanted to acquire enough competence to be seen as a person from the cultural background implied by my last name. All my life I had been surrounded by people ethnically or racially different from me, and while not identifying with them, I had tried to blur the distinctions and fade into the background.

From early adolescence through middle age, I wasn't able to envision a viable alternative to hiding. Luckily, though very late in life, I have finally begun to fashion an identity that other people can use to get a handle on me. Given my history, I am very aware of the limitations entailed in playing this game. Evaluating in terms of essences, in my opinion, is psychologically and philosophically unacceptable. We are all becoming; if that makes it more difficult to identify one another, so be it.

Made in the USA
San Bernardino, CA
18 May 2014